OPPOSING
VIEWPOINTS®
SERIES

Criminal Justice

Other Books of Related Interest:

Opposing Viewpoints Series
Civil Liberties

Cybercrime

The Death Penalty

At Issue Series
Alternatives to Prisons

Guns and Crime

Tasers

Current Controversies Series
Espionage and Intelligence

Family Violence

Search and Seizure

"Congress shall make no law . . . abridging the freedom of speech, or of the press."

First Amendment to the US Constitution

The basic foundation of our democracy is the First Amendment guarantee of freedom of expression. The Opposing Viewpoints series is dedicated to the concept of this basic freedom and the idea that it is more important to practice it than to enshrine it.

OPPOSING VIEWPOINTS® SERIES

I Criminal Justice

Noël Merino, Book Editor

GREENHAVEN PRESS
A part of Gale, Cengage Learning

GALE
CENGAGE Learning·

Detroit • New York • San Francisco • New Haven, Conn • Waterville, Maine • London

Elizabeth Des Chenes, *Director, Publishing Solutions*

© 2013 Greenhaven Press, a part of Gale, Cengage Learning.

Gale and Greenhaven Press are registered trademarks used herein under license.

For more information, contact:
Greenhaven Press
27500 Drake Rd.
Farmington Hills, MI 48331-3535
Or you can visit our Internet site at gale.cengage.com

For product information and technology assistance, contact us at

Gale Customer Support, 1-800-877-4253
For permission to use material from this text or product, submit all requests online at www.cengage.com/permissions

Further permissions questions can be emailed to permissionrequest@cengage.com

Articles in Greenhaven Press anthologies are often edited for length to meet page requirements. In addition, original titles of these works are changed to clearly present the main thesis and to explicitly indicate the author's opinion. Every effort is made to ensure that Greenhaven Press accurately reflects the original intent of the authors. Every effort has been made to trace the owners of copyrighted material.

Cover Image copyright © David Chasey/Photodisc/Getty.

LIBRARY OF CONGRESS CATALOGING-IN-PUBLICATION DATA

Criminal Justice / [edited by] Noël Merino.
  p. cm. -- (Opposing viewpoints)
Summary: "Criminal Justice: Opposing Viewpoints is the leading source for libraries and classrooms in need of current-issue materials. The viewpoints are selected from a wide range of highly respected sources and publications"-- Provided by publisher.
  Includes bibliographical references and index.
  ISBN 978-0-7377-6306-5 (hardback) -- ISBN 978-0-7377-6307-2 (paperback)
  1. Criminal justice, Administration of--United States. I. Merino, Noël.
  KF9223.C748 2012
  364.973--dc23
                                                              2012021681

Printed in the United States of America
1 2 3 4 5 6 7 16 15 14 13 12

Contents

Chapter 3: Should Sentencing Laws Be Reformed?

Chapter 4: What Rights Should Be a Part of the Criminal Justice System?

Why Consider Opposing Viewpoints?

> *"The only way in which a human being can make some approach to knowing the whole of a subject is by hearing what can be said about it by persons of every variety of opinion and studying all modes in which it can be looked at by every character of mind. No wise man ever acquired his wisdom in any mode but this."*
>
> John Stuart Mill

In our media-intensive culture it is not difficult to find differing opinions. Thousands of newspapers and magazines and dozens of radio and television talk shows resound with differing points of view. The difficulty lies in deciding which opinion to agree with and which "experts" seem the most credible. The more inundated we become with differing opinions and claims, the more essential it is to hone critical reading and thinking skills to evaluate these ideas. Opposing Viewpoints books address this problem directly by presenting stimulating debates that can be used to enhance and teach these skills. The varied opinions contained in each book examine many different aspects of a single issue. While examining these conveniently edited opposing views, readers can develop critical thinking skills such as the ability to compare and contrast authors' credibility, facts, argumentation styles, use of persuasive techniques, and other stylistic tools. In short, the Opposing Viewpoints Series is an ideal way to attain the higher-level thinking and reading skills so essential in a culture of diverse and contradictory opinions.

In addition to providing a tool for critical thinking, Opposing Viewpoints books challenge readers to question their own strongly held opinions and assumptions. Most people form their opinions on the basis of upbringing, peer pressure, and personal, cultural, or professional bias. By reading carefully balanced opposing views, readers must directly confront new ideas as well as the opinions of those with whom they disagree. This is not to argue simplistically that everyone who reads opposing views will—or should—change his or her opinion. Instead, the series enhances readers' understanding of their own views by encouraging confrontation with opposing ideas. Careful examination of others' views can lead to the readers' understanding of the logical inconsistencies in their own opinions, perspective on why they hold an opinion, and the consideration of the possibility that their opinion requires further evaluation.

Evaluating Other Opinions

To ensure that this type of examination occurs, Opposing Viewpoints books present all types of opinions. Prominent spokespeople on different sides of each issue as well as well-known professionals from many disciplines challenge the reader. An additional goal of the series is to provide a forum for other, less known, or even unpopular viewpoints. The opinion of an ordinary person who has had to make the decision to cut off life support from a terminally ill relative, for example, may be just as valuable and provide just as much insight as a medical ethicist's professional opinion. The editors have two additional purposes in including these less known views. One, the editors encourage readers to respect others' opinions—even when not enhanced by professional credibility. It is only by reading or listening to and objectively evaluating others' ideas that one can determine whether they are worthy of consideration. Two, the inclusion of such viewpoints encourages the important critical thinking skill of objectively evaluating an author's credentials and bias. This evaluation will illuminate an author's reasons for taking a particular stance on an issue and will aid in readers' evaluation of the author's ideas.

It is our hope that these books will give readers a deeper understanding of the issues debated and an appreciation of the complexity of even seemingly simple issues when good and honest people disagree. This awareness is particularly important in a democratic society such as ours in which people enter into public debate to determine the common good. Those with whom one disagrees should not be regarded as enemies but rather as people whose views deserve careful examination and may shed light on one's own.

Thomas Jefferson once said that "difference of opinion leads to inquiry, and inquiry to truth." Jefferson, a broadly educated man, argued that "if a nation expects to be ignorant and free . . . it expects what never was and never will be." As individuals and as a nation, it is imperative that we consider the opinions of others and examine them with skill and discernment. The Opposing Viewpoints series is intended to help readers achieve this goal.

David L. Bender and Bruno Leone,
Founders

Introduction

> "Americans' confidence in the U.S. criminal justice system is muted, with as many Americans expressing low confidence as high confidence."
>
> —Lydia Saad,
> "Americans Express Mixed Confidence in Criminal Justice System,"
> Gallup, July 11, 2011

The criminal justice system in the United States is a combination of the laws against criminal behavior and the institutions that enforce those laws. Such institutions include law enforcement, the courts (including prosecutors and defense attorneys), and correctional programs and facilities. The purpose of the criminal justice system is to deter and control crime. Whether or not the laws and institutions are successful at deterring and controlling crime is an issue of much controversy and dispute, and criticism of the US criminal justice system comes from many different perspectives.

Whereas federal law is the same throughout the United States, laws defining criminal behavior vary widely among states and local municipalities. For example, in the cities of Butte, Montana, and New Orleans, Louisiana, the possession and consumption of alcoholic beverages in open containers is allowed by those of drinking age. Cities such as Portland, Oregon, and New York City, however, do not allow possession and consumption of alcoholic beverages in open containers, and violation of the law can lead to criminal prosecution. Another example where laws vary is that of the age of consent for sexual activity. Whereas the age is sixteen in Minnesota, it is eighteen in California. Although the specific criminal charges vary by circumstance, when an adult has sexual relations with a minor under the age of consent, there is the possibility of being charged with rape. It is up to individuals to be aware of local law and to follow it, regardless of where one resides. The difference in laws illustrates different approaches to criminalizing behavior and different beliefs about the efficacy of laws in affecting public safety.

Law enforcement is a function of state and municipal governments, and the most common law enforcement agency is the police. Federal law enforcement deals only with crimes that are against the US government, crimes committed while engaged in government duties, and crimes committed that involve the crossing of state lines. The effectiveness of the police in controlling criminal activity depends a great deal on the public's level of trust. Police departments that are seen as a danger to certain members of society rather than as a help will not be called in when needed, and criminal behavior may go unreported and unpunished. At the end of 2011, the US Department of Justice released a highly critical report after an investigation into police brutality in Seattle, saying that police have engaged in a pattern of unnecessary or excessive force that amounts to a violation of constitutional rights. Some say the police brutality is the result of a failure of community members to interact with police. According to Casey McNerthney, writing in *Seattle 911—A Police and Crime Blog* on February 27, 2012, "Multiple juvenile shooting deaths . . . haven't been solved—and hindered by people who won't talk to police." In other words, the effectiveness of law enforcement in deterring and controlling crime depends on the ability of law enforcement to gain the community's trust.

Federal law enforcement agencies include the US Marshals Service (USMS); the Federal Bureau of Investigation (FBI); the Drug Enforcement Administration (DEA); the Bureau of Alcohol, Tobacco, Firearms and Explosives (ATF); US Border Patrol (USBP), and the Department of Homeland Security (DHS). Since the passage of the USA PATRIOT Act in October 2001, federal investigative powers have been expanded dramatically, causing some to worry that federal law enforcement is overstepping its bounds. Questions about federal law enforcement's proper boundaries abound; for example, Arizona passed an immigration law in 2010 requiring that local police take on the role of enforcing immigration laws, a task traditionally under the auspices of federal agencies such as USBP. The US Court of Appeals for the Ninth Circuit blocked the section of the law that would have required Arizona law enforcement to check the immigration status of suspects, saying that the state had overstepped its authority. Judge Richard A. Paez wrote in his majority opinion in *Arizona v. United States* on April 11, 2011, that "contrary to the State's view, we simply are not persuaded that Arizona has the authority to unilaterally transform state and local law enforcement officers into a state-controlled DHS force to carry out its declared policy of attrition." The US Supreme Court heard the arguments for overturning this ruling in June 2012. Commentators speculated that the case might help delineate more clearly the role of federal law enforcement. Although the court struck down several key parts of the Arizona law, it left standing the controversial provision that requires law enforcement officers to check immigration status of those they detain and suspect of being in the country illegally.

The correctional programs of the United States include imprisonment and probation, and the correctional facilities include jails and prisons. Correctional programs exist to respond to violations of the criminal law. When a person has been convicted of a criminal act, the punishment may include imprisonment or probation. There are various justifications for punishment, and the type of punishment meted out depends upon which justifications are endorsed. One of the main reasons for punishing criminal behavior is deterrence— both to prevent criminals from re-offending and to prevent would-be criminals from committing criminal acts in the first place. According to deterrence theories, the ultimate deterrence for a convicted criminal is, of course, incapacitation either through incarceration or the death penalty. Another theory of punishment holds that punishment should rehabilitate criminals, making them less likely to re-offend. In contrast, the retributive theory sees punishment itself as helping to restore some justice by ensuring the criminal suffers a loss. Differing opinions of how prison inmates should be treated stem from these different theories. Outrage over the purchase of new forty-two-inch flat-screen televisions at the Allegheny County Jail in Pittsburgh, Pennsylvania, in 2011 caused a member of the county jail oversight board to respond to critics by saying, "The point of being in jail is not to mistreat people or make them feel worse and resentful." In fact, proponents of the retributive theory of justice think that is precisely the point. Determining how correctional programs should function depends greatly on the justification for the punishment.

In *Opposing Viewpoints: Criminal Justice*, several authorities examine how well the criminal laws and institutions of the US criminal justice system are working. Critics and commentators take a variety of viewpoints on the subject of the American criminal justice system in the following chapters: Does the Criminal Justice System Need Reform?, What Is the State of the Incarceration System in the United States?, Should Sentencing Laws Be Reformed?, and What Rights Should Be a Part of the Criminal Justice System? Together, the authors in this volume seek to answer the questions of whether all Americans receive justice at the hands of law enforcement, the courts, and correctional facilities and whether or not the justice system is making the United States safer and more secure.

CHAPTER 1

Does the Criminal Justice System Need Reform?

Chapter Preface

Two of the authors in this chapter, Sasha Abramsky and Nastassia Walsh, debate the efficacy of problem-solving courts—particularly drug courts—as an alternative to traditional criminal courts. Both agree that society needs to deal with drug addiction and drug-related crime in some manner. The drug courts endorsed by Abramsky are one way to do this, and drug treatment in the community as endorsed by Walsh is another alternative. But other commentators, such as Radley Balko, argue that neither of these methods addresses one of the main avenues for criminal justice reform through changing drug laws so that fewer criminals are created in the first place. Balko argues that "drug laws undermine order by creating criminal enterprises in low-income communities that wouldn't exist without a black market, by enticing cops into corruption, and by locking up millions of people for consensual crimes, imposing on them all the limitations that come with incarceration and a felony record."

Detractors argue that current drug policy creates more criminals because of the illicit nature of drugs in the first place. This view was endorsed by several international organizations in a 2011 report by Count the Costs, titled "The War on Drugs: Creating Crime, Enriching Criminals." The report states, "It is clear that a significant proportion of the street crime and sex work blighting urban environments has its roots in the war on drugs. These problems result from the criminally controlled supply and dramatically inflated prices the drug war has created." Proponents for drug legalization argue that with supply available and prices lowered, drug users would not be pushed into a life of crime. And, as Balko suggests, police would not be enticed into corruption from the drug trade.

The second way that current US drug laws create more criminals is simply due to the fact that drugs such as marijuana, cocaine, and heroin are illegal, thus making anyone who uses or possesses them a criminal. Yet surely the argument that laws create criminals alone is not a reason for repeal; eliminating laws against murder and theft would do this as well. But if such laws do not serve the same social purpose that laws against murder and theft do, then their justification is in doubt. More and more Americans of all political stripes are coming to consider decriminalization of drugs, at least for marijuana. The editors of the conservative *National Review* on May 19, 2009, wrote: "In the calculus of public good, the costs of marijuana interdiction and the invasive paternalism associated with it outweigh the costs that are imposed by marijuana use." They claim, "A marijuana habit generally will not interfere with one's ability to find and keep gainful employment, for instance, or to otherwise conduct one's life independently and productively; a felony conviction will."

Whereas drug laws regarding marijuana have softened somewhat around the country, especially for the use of medical marijuana, there are few signs that laws prohibiting other drugs—such as cocaine and heroin—are likely to be minimized anytime soon. And, even with marijuana, there is far from a consensus on the issue. The US Drug Enforcement Administration (DEA) itself says in its 2010 publication "Speaking Out Against Drug Legalization" that legalizing drugs will have an effect on crime rates: "Criminals won't stop being criminals if we make drugs legal. Individuals who have chosen to pursue a life of crime and violence aren't likely to change course, get legitimate jobs, and become honest, tax-paying citizens just because we legalize drugs." Furthermore, the DEA denies that drug laws lack justification, claiming, "Drug use is regulated, and access to drugs is controlled, because drugs can be harmful."

There are numerous proposals for reforming the US criminal justice system. They range from proposals to reform the laws, to ideas for reforming the courts, to suggestions for reform to correctional programs and facilities. In this chapter, a few of these proposals are debated, including suggested reforms to the federal criminal justice system, the advent of problem-solving courts, and the need for reform due to racial discrimination.

| "[Terrorism] cases have showcased just
how effectively the system still works."

The Federal Criminal Justice System Works Well for Trying Terrorists

Karen J. Greenberg

In the following viewpoint, Karen J. Greenberg argues that despite attempts by the administrations of the last decade to avoid the courts for trying accused terrorists, the federal court system is effective for the trials of those charged with terrorism. Greenberg contends that the trend toward punishing those charged with terrorism prior to trial is both disturbing and unwarranted. She claims that recent terrorism cases in the federal criminal justice system show that the system works. Greenberg is director of the Center on National Security, a visiting fellow at Fordham Law School, and author of The Least Worst Place: Guantanamo's First 100 Days.

As you read, consider the following questions:

1. What statistic does Greenberg cite in support of her view that the military commissions system has a record of underperformance?

Karen J. Greenberg, "Crisis of Confidence: How Washington Lost Faith in America's Courts," TomDispatch.com, August 21, 2011. Copyright © 2011 by Karen J. Greenberg. All rights reserved. Reproduced by permission.

2. Greenberg claims that whistleblower Thomas Drake suffered what specific punishment prior to his trial?

3. The author charges that success in terrorism prosecutions is defined in what way by the Obama administration, just as it was by the Bush administration?

As the 10th anniversary of 9/11 [referring to the September 11, 2001, terrorist attacks on the United States] approaches, the unexpected extent of the damage Americans have done to themselves and their institutions is coming into better focus. The event that "changed everything" did turn out to change Washington in ways more startling than most people realize. On terrorism and national security, to take an obvious (if seldom commented upon) example, the confidence of the U.S. government seems to have been severely, perhaps irreparably, shaken when it comes to that basic and essential American institution: the courts.

Avoidance of the Court System

If, in fact, we are a "nation of laws," you wouldn't know it from Washington's actions over the past few years. Nothing spoke more strikingly to that loss of faith, to our country's increasing incapacity for meeting violence with the law, than the widely hailed decision to kill rather than capture Osama bin Laden.

Clearly, a key factor in that decision was a growing belief, widely shared within the national security establishment, that none of our traditional or even newly created tribunals, civilian or military, could have handled a bin Laden trial. Washington's faith went solely to Navy SEALs zooming into another country's sovereign airspace on a moonless night on a mission to assassinate bin Laden, whether he offered the slightest resistance or not. It evidently seemed so much easier to the top officials overseeing the operation—and so much less messy—than bringing a confessed mass murderer into a court-room in, or even anywhere near, the United States.

The decision to kill bin Laden on sight rather than capture him and bring him to trial followed hard on the heels of an ignominious [President Barack] Obama administration climb-down on its plan to try the "mastermind" of the 9/11 attacks, Khalid Sheikh Mohammed, or KSM, in a federal court in New York City. Captured in Pakistan in May 2003 and transferred to Guantánamo [Bay detention center] in 2006, his proposed trial was, under political pressure, returned to a military venue earlier this year [2011].

Given the extraordinary record of underperformance by the military commissions system—only six convictions in 10 years—it's hard to escape the conclusion that the United States has little faith in its ability to put on trial a man assumedly responsible for murdering thousands.

And don't assume that these high-level examples of avoiding the court system are just knotty exceptions that prove the rule. There is evidence that the administration's skepticism and faint-heartedness when it comes to using the judicial system risks becoming pervasive.

The Impact of the War on Terror

Needless to say, this backing away from courts of law as institutions appropriate for handling terrorism suspects began in the [George W.] Bush–[Dick] Cheney years. Top officials in the Bush administration believed civilian courts to be far too weak for the global war on terror they had declared. This, as they saw it, was largely because those courts would supposedly gift foreign terrorist suspects with a slew of American legal rights that might act as so many get-out-of-jail-free cards.

As a result, despite a shining record of terrorism convictions in civilian courts in the 1990s—including the prosecutions of those responsible for the 1993 attempt to take down a tower of the World Trade Center—President Bush issued a military order on November 13, 2001, that established the court-less contours of public debate to come. It mandated that non-American terrorists captured abroad would be put under the jurisdiction of the Pentagon, not the federal court system. This was "war," after all, and the enemy had to be confronted by fighting men, not those sticklers for due process, civilian judges and juries.

The federal courts have, of course, continued to try American citizens and residents (and even, in a few cases, individuals captured abroad) in terror cases of all sorts—with an 87% conviction rate for both violent and nonviolent crimes. In fact, 2010 was a banner year for terrorism prosecutions when it came to American citizens and residents, and 2011 is following suit. As could have been predicted, in the vast majority of these cases—all the ones that mattered—there were convictions.

A Policy of Punishment Before Trial

You might think, then, that the courts had proved their mettle against mounting criticism and distrust of a system said to be insufficiently harsh. And initially Obama's Department of Justice defended civilian courts as resilient and flexible enough to try terror cases.

But that didn't last. Recently, the Obama administration has reinforced a policy (begun under President Bush) which offers an ominous new twist on American justice: punishment before trial. It has, for example, relied upon various extreme methods of pretrial isolation—including a version of restrictive orders known as Special Administrative Measures, or SAMs—that reek of punitiveness and have often caused severe psychological deterioration in suspects awaiting trial on terrorism charges. The most noteworthy case of this is Syed Fahad Hashmi's. An American citizen arrested while studying in England, Hashmi had allowed an acquaintance, Mohammed Junaid Babar, to stay in his apartment for two weeks. Babar, who testified against Hashmi and was later released, allegedly had socks, ponchos, and raingear intended for al-Qaeda in his luggage and allegedly used Hashmi's cell phone to call terrorist conspirators. Hashmi, accused of "material support" for al-Qaeda, was kept under SAMs for three years without trial—until he finally pled guilty.

The urge to punish before a verdict comes in reflects the same deep-seated conviction that the U.S. court system is simply not to be trusted to do its job. Two recent cases—that of whistleblowers Thomas Drake and Bradley Manning—illustrate how, in cases where national security is believed to be at stake, Obama-era pretrial treatment has taken up the distrust of the courts, civilian or military, that characterized the Bush years.

Two Cases of Punishment Preceding Trial

Drake, an executive for the National Security Agency (NSA), became a whistleblower over what he considered mistaken policy decisions about an ill-performing data-sifting program which, among other things, he thought squandered taxpayer money. Subsequently, he revealed his disagreement with the agency's warrantless wiretapping program, which he believed overstepped legal boundaries. Charged initially with violating the Espionage Act and threatened with a draconian 35-year jail sentence, Drake finally pled this past June to a misdemeanor count of "exceeding the authorized use of a government computer."

In Drake's four-year saga, his pre-punishment took the form not of pretrial detention but of the destruction of his livelihood. He was initially fired from the NSA and from the National Defense University position to which the NSA had assigned him. Once indicted in 2010, he was forced to resign from a subsequent teaching post at Strayer University. All told, the formal and informal hounding of Drake resulted in the loss of his jobs and pension, as well as $82,000 in legal costs.

Ultimately, Drake was sentenced to a year's probation and 240 hours of mandatory community service. By that time, he had been ruined financially and professionally, thanks to the government's disparagement of him and the multiyear delay between its accusations and the lodging of formal charges against him. Drake now works at an Apple Store. In other words, well before the government took its chances in court, Thomas Drake was punished.

Another highly publicized case where punishment preceded trial has been the mistreatment of Army Private Bradley Manning while in military custody in a Marine brig in Quantico, Virginia, awaiting charges. The Obama administration believes he turned over a trove of secret military and State Department documents to the website WikiLeaks. Following his arrest, Manning was kept in subhuman conditions. He was forced to sleep naked and to strip for daily inspections, though as news about his situation generated bad publicity, he was eventually allowed to sleep in a "tear-proof" gown.

There is something deeply disturbing about the very different ways Manning and Drake were pre-punished by the government—both directly in the case of Manning and indirectly in the case of Drake—before being given due process of any kind. Like bin Laden's killing, both cases reflect an unspoken worry in Washington that our courts will prove insufficiently ruthless and so incapable of giving the "obviously guilty" what they "obviously" deserve.

Justice in the Courts

As it turns out, the judicial system hasn't taken the government's new attitude lying down. Various judges and juries have, in fact, shown themselves to be unfazed by both public and governmental pressures and have, in terror and national security cases, demonstrated signs of balance and of a concern for justice, rather than being driven by a blind sense of revenge.

In the past year, there has been an unprecedented number of high-profile terrorism trials. All have resulted in convictions, which have nonetheless not reflected the unstinting harshness that critics of court-centered counterterrorism insist upon. In the case of Ahmed Ghailani, the sole Guantánamo detainee to face trial in the nation's criminal justice system, the jury, having done its work of assessing the evidence, acquitted the defendant on 284 of 285 counts, including all the murder charges associated with the 1998 bombings of the U.S. embassies in Kenya and Tanzania. On the single count on which he was convicted, however, Ghailani was given a life sentence without parole.

Meanwhile, a high-profile terrorism case—that of Tahawwur Rana—ended in a jury acquittal on its most serious charge. Rana had been accused of cooperating in the 2008 terrorist attacks in Mumbai, India, which resulted in the deaths of more than 160 individuals. The jury found Rana guilty of material support, but not of helping to coordinate the attack.

These cases and others like them have, of course, been fodder for all the usual critics who consider anything but a 100% conviction rate on all charges in all cases to be a sure sign not of the justice system's strength, but of its fundamental weakness. And yet, such cases have showcased just how effectively the system still works, in a more nuanced way than in the previous near-decade, as well as in a subtler and more just way than Washington has managed to approximate over that same period. Despite the fears, pressures, and scare tactics that are entangled with all such terror cases, we now have living proof that juries can think for themselves, and guilt can be a partial matter, rather than a Washington slam dunk.

Growing Expressions of Judicial Dissatisfaction

Of late, federal judges on such cases also seem to have been signaling to the government's representatives that they must be more restrained in their approach to national security cases, both in and out of court. In late June, for instance, during the sentencing of three of the men convicted of conspiring to bomb two synagogues in Riverdale, New York, and to launch a Stinger missile aimed at aircraft over Newburgh's Air National Guard base, Judge Colleen McMahon struck back at the government's case. "I believe beyond a shadow of a doubt," she said, "that there would have been no crime here except the government instigated it, planned it, and brought it to fruition. That does not mean that there was no crime. The jury concluded that you were not entrapped, and I see no basis to overturn their verdict."

In the Drake case, Judge Richard Bennett was similarly distraught about the evident excesses in the government's approach. At sentencing for the single minor count to which Drake agreed to plead, the judge bluntly refused to impose the $50,000 fine the prosecution was pushing for on the grounds that punishment had already been administered—prior to the court process. "There has been financial devastation wrought upon this defendant," said Bennett, "that far exceeds any fine that can be imposed by me. And I'm not going to add to that in any way. And it's very obvious to me in terms of some of the irritation I've expressed . . . not only my concern over the delay in this case . . . [but also the prosecution's] inability to explain . . . the delay in this case . . . I think that somebody somewhere in the U.S. government has to say . . . that the American public deserves better than this."

In the recent jury decisions, as in the growing expressions of judicial dissatisfaction, an optimist might find signs that the system is finally starting to right itself. On the other hand, a pessimist might come to the conclusion that the government will, in the future, simply put even more energy into avoiding the court system.

The bottom line is that the Obama administration, like its predecessor, defines success in terrorism prosecutions not by assessing whether or not due process and fair verdicts are administered, but solely in terms of what they deem proper punishment for those accused of violating national security—especially when doing so minimizes partisan political clashes. By refusing to rein in its evident distrust of the judicial system when it comes to national security, the government is perpetuating a legal landscape that, to this day, lies in the shadow of Osama bin Laden.

"Studies have repeatedly shown that these courts save money and prevent future offenses."

May It Please the Court

Sasha Abramsky

In the following viewpoint, Sasha Abramsky argues that problem-solving courts, which include drug courts and health courts, pro-vide attractive alternatives to incarceration. Abramsky contends that research has shown that these alternative courts save money and reduce recidivism. Abramsky claims that increasing the number of problem-solving courts should be a priority in re-forming the criminal justice system. Abramsky is a journalist and a senior fellow at Demos, a multi-issue organization.

As you read, consider the following questions:

1. The author claims that the San Francisco court system has calculated that for every ninety cents invested in problem-solving courts, how much is saved?

2. According to Abramsky, approximately how many problem-solving courts are there nationwide?

Sasha Abramsky, "May It Please the Court," *American Prospect*, January/February 2011, vol. 22, no. 1, pp. A14–A15. Copyright © 2011 by The American Prospect. All rights re-served. Reproduced by permission.

3. The author claims that a 2008 study determined that how many individuals may be eligible for problem-solving courts?

Inside a nondescript building on Polk Street in San Francisco's troubled Tenderloin district, an experimental court is trying to sort out the lives of the accused. Known as the Community Justice Center, the court regularly sees prostitutes, thieves, alcoholics, drug users and dealers, and mentally ill and homeless people primarily for nonviolent offenses. The average defendant has been arrested locally eight times. Instead of sending offenders straight to an overcrowded and expensive jail, presiding Judge Loretta Giorgi tries to connect them with social services that might finally end their downward spiral.

On a recent fall day, Giorgi asked a middle-aged defendant to attend drug-rehab sessions, admonished a young, tattooed man for sleeping through counseling sessions, and ordered another defendant to undergo more frequent urinalysis. The court makes these mandates easy to fulfill: The Polk Street center houses not only the court but also social services, including case-management, housing-assistance, and onsite support groups. The defendants are given highly personalized and structured plans of action designed to distance them from crime, drugs, and alcohol during their time at the court, which can last from months to more than a year. Many are also required to perform community service.

If an offender successfully completes counseling and substance-abuse treatment, Giorgi will often cut the original sentence or probation period, or the district attorney's office will reduce or dismiss the charges. After a graduation ceremony, in which defendants receive a diploma to the applause of the courtroom, some can go on to apply for and emerge from the system with a clean record. Failing the program, however, means that they will likely serve the original sentence behind bars. Since opening its doors in March 2009, the center has seen 2,950 defendants.

"We're taking the hardest-to-serve cases and getting the most success," says Lisa Lightman, director of San Francisco's Collaborative Courts, which oversees 11 nontraditional courts, including the Community Justice Center. In May 2009, her office published a study showing that mentally ill offenders who completed treatment through the city's Behavioral Health Court were 55 percent less likely to be charged with a new violent offense than were their peers who had not been through the program. Overall, BHC clients were 26 percent less likely to be charged with any offense after finishing treatment. Drug-court participants were also far less likely to be charged with new crimes and were arrested fewer times in the three years following their original arrest than were addicts who did not go through the specialized court process. There are cost-saving benefits, as well. The San Francisco court system has calculated that by the third year, the behavioral courts were saving $1 for every 90 cents invested.

"You see folks who have been functioning at a very, very low level for a long time," Giorgi says. "We see victory in even small things. If they're committing crimes once every six months instead of once every month, that's a success. And then there are big things. We see amazing changes in addicts who've turned their lives around."

These nontraditional courts are formally known as problem-solving courts. They have emerged over the past two decades as an alternative to sending habitual offenders to prison or jail yet again. While their institutional origins can be traced back to diversion programs created in the 1960s, their specific carrot-and-stick approach is more recent, as is their embrace of fairly stringent supervision requirements for clients. These measures include regular urinalysis and sometimes even electronic monitoring; the reliance on evidence-based treatment and rehabilitation means problem-solving courts tend to produce better results.

The idea is to provide a combination of punishment and treatment that lowers recidivism and increases participation in and completion of drug- and mental-health treatment programs. Though experimental in their efforts to reduce recidivism, these courts have the same authority as their traditional counterparts. Critics argue that the courts force some offenders into unnecessary treatment and that at-risk individuals shouldn't have to wait until an arrest to gain access to needed social services. Yet studies have repeatedly shown that these courts save money and prevent future offenses. In an era in which one in 100 adult Americans is incarcerated, advocates of problem-solving courts face an incredible challenge: reproducing those outcomes not just for tens of thousands but hundreds of thousands, if not millions, of offenders nationally.

The first drug court in the country was founded in Miami in 1989 with the intent of diverting low-level, nonviolent drug offenders into treatment. Prosecutors had to approve the diversion, and defendants were told they should expect to spend at least a year in treatment. Four years later, a broader alternative model was pioneered in New York, when the Midtown Community Court began hearing misdemeanor and low-end felony cases, involving crimes like shoplifting, graffiti, fare beating, and prostitution. The goal was to reduce the number of New Yorkers entering jail and prison. In the decades since, the number of specialized courts, including ones that handle domestic-violence and mental-health cases, has mushroomed. There are now more than 3,000 courts nationwide, according to the New York–based nonprofit organization Center for Court Innovation.

Some critics of drug-law reform argue that the courts are coercive. The National Association of Criminal Defense Lawyers has blasted the model, calling the courts "conviction mills" for forcing defendants to plead guilty to charges simply

Criminal Activity in Offenders in Prior Six Months, With and Without Drug Court

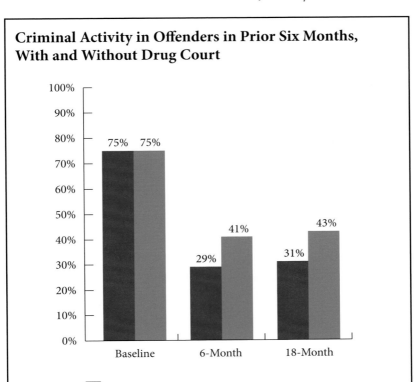

TAKEN FROM: Shelli B. Rossman, John K. Roman, Janine M. Zweig, et al., "The Multi-Site Adult Drug Court Evaluation: The Impact of Drug Courts," Urban Institute, November 2011.

to access treatment programs. Judges and attorneys, critics say, are also aggressive about securing pleas and enrolling offenders in treatment programs, including medication regimens and drug rehab, which potentially infringe on a defendant's due process and personal rights.

These are legitimate concerns, and many in the field are trying to address them both by engaging defense lawyers and counselors more actively in discussions about what to do with clients who aren't succeeding in the program and by emphasizing the use of short stints in jail rather than sending offenders back to prison for noncompliant behavior.

While advocates remain sensitive to such criticism, they can also point to consistent research showing that the alternative model, at least on the small scale at which it is currently employed, is successful at reducing recidivism and saving taxpayers' money.

To develop viable and safe alternatives to incarceration for a range of offenders, the courts use risk-assessment models to gauge the most appropriate approach. The model generally evaluates education level, age, drug addiction, and when the criminal behavior first began. Most states have their own risk-assessment tools for a range of defendants, including for juvenile and domestic-violence cases. In mental-health courts, offenders are diagnosed, and their history of medication compliance is reviewed.

The assessment is an evidence-based method of achieving the best outcome for the offender and the system, and as in San Francisco, many of the courts have impressive track records in reducing recidivism as well as trial and incarceration costs. A 2007 study from the RAND Corporation showed that defendants in Allegheny County, Pennsylvania's mental-health courts re-offended at a lower rate than their peers and that the savings associated with this increased over time, suggesting graduates weren't staying away from crime only in the short term but were changing their behavior long term.

There's no average cost to creating and running a problem-solving court; some have minimal expenses while others require hundreds of thousands of dollars to maintain annually. Greg Berman, director of the Center for Court Innovation, says the costs depend on existing courtroom infrastructure and supervision needs.

Even with those expenditures, cost-benefit analyses by the National Institute of Justice have concluded that problem-solving courts save taxpayers about $1,300 in treatment and other costs and between $6,000 and $12,000 per participant in reduced costs associated with recidivism and victimization. There are other convincing studies, including a 2004 report from the National Drug Court Institute that found treating drug-court clients was significantly cheaper than incarcerating them.

In the wake of such research, the Conference of Chief Justices, a national group comprising senior state-level judges, has endorsed expanding state networks of problem-solving courts to make them an integral part of the court process rather than an on-the-margins experiment.

And that's what they are at the moment. Data show that the courts reach only a sliver of the offenders who could benefit from such an intervention. A 2008 Urban Institute study found that only 55,000 individuals had been to drug court out of an estimated 1.5 million who might be eligible.

Berman believes in spreading the successful practices of problem-solving courts, including through the conversion of traditional courts. Of course, this requires providing judges with the right training—a daunting task since the curriculum for standard skills-based seminars is determined state by state. Jane Spinak, a Columbia University professor of law and co-chair of the Task Force on Family Courts in New York City, also worries about the role of judges in problem-solving courts. Many judges, she says, don't have the background to act as de facto social workers to drug-addicted, mentally ill, and otherwise troubled defendants who come before their benches.

Another obstacle to expansion, Berman says, is the wildly varying eligibility guidelines. These are decided county by county and often after local judges, defense attorneys, and prosecutors have debated the terms. Berman doesn't want to stifle local innovation but said the federal government, through the Bureau of Justice, could use its influence in funding projects and providing technical assistance as well as its power to issue new regulations to encourage local courts to be as broad-minded as possible in determining eligibility.

Despite these challenges, problem-solving courts remain essential to reforming the justice system. The Bureau of Justice set aside $45 million for drug courts in fiscal year 2010 and offers technical assistance to fledging and established mental-health courts. "There's a real hunger for alternatives to incarceration," Berman says. "There's a real hunger for programs that can marshal data for their efficacy. There's a moment to be seized."

> *"While drug courts may be a better jus-
> tice system option than incarceration,
> they are still a justice system approach
> to a public health issue."*

Drug Courts Are Not a Positive Reform to the Criminal Justice System

Nastassia Walsh

*In the following viewpoint, Nastassia Walsh argues that drug
courts are not the most effective way to deal with people charged
with drug offenses. Walsh claims that there is no reason for drug
treatment to be administered by the justice system and that drug
courts are not the best way to improve public safety. She argues
that money spent on drug courts could be more effectively spent
by focusing on community treatment and prevention initiatives
outside the justice system. Walsh is policy analyst for the Council
of State Governments' Justice Center and former research man-
ager at the Justice Policy Institute.*

As you read, consider the following questions:

1. According to Walsh, what percentage of admissions to
   state prisons in 2008 were for drug offenses?

2. The author claims that Washington State Institute for Public Policy reported that what kind of programs reduced crime by about 18 percent?

3. Walsh claims that less than what percentage of all substance abuse and addiction spending is for prevention, treatment, and research?

The 2009 U.S. National Survey on Drug Use and Health revealed that 21.8 million people—8.7 percent of the population over age 12—reported using illicit drugs in the month prior to being surveyed. About 7.8 million people surveyed indicated they needed treatment; this is more than the prevalence of lung, breast and prostate cancer combined. As addiction is a disease, an appropriate approach to a public health issue of this magnitude would be to substantially increase funding for treatment in communities. But this has not been the case.

A Public Health Issue

Instead of providing treatment for people with addictions, over the last few decades there has been a war on people who use drugs, fought through the criminal justice system. Police made 1.6 million arrests for drug offenses in 2009; of these, more than four in five were for possession rather than sales of illegal drugs. In 2008, 29 percent of all admissions to state prisons—194,000—were for drug offenses.

The explosion of prison populations, due in part to increasing numbers of people convicted of drug offenses, led some states and localities to explore alternatives to drug incarceration. One such alternative that was developed in the late 1980s was the drug court. As originally envisioned, drug courts would be a new model that would reduce the number of people in prison for drug offenses, help people with addictions, and improve public safety. Over 55,000 people enter drug courts annually.

While drug courts may be a better justice system option than incarceration, they are still a justice system approach to a public health issue. Drug courts also are not the most effective way to help people who are struggling with addiction, and in many ways, only serve to "widen the net" of U.S. criminal justice control, which now stands at about 7 million people either incarcerated or on probation or parole. . . .

Unnecessary Involvement by the Justice System

A perception among drug court supporters is that drug courts are the most effective way to work with people with addictions who come into contact with the justice system. This is partially based on a belief that people need the threat of sanctions to be motivated into treatment. But national data and research from people who actually provide treatment tell a different story.

Front-end treatment for people before they become involved in the justice system can be even more effective than treatment through the justice system, which includes drug courts, and it improves public safety by reducing the "collateral damage" that addiction can cause to communities.

Claims that people with substance abuse problems need the added push of judicial supervision to succeed are not supported [by the] data. Statistics from the Substance Abuse and Mental Health Services Administration (SAMHSA) Treatment Episode Data Set (TEDS) show little difference in terms of success for people who are referred to treatment by criminal justice agencies and those from other sources. About 49 percent of people who are referred to treatment by criminal justice agencies complete treatment and another 13 percent are transferred to another level of care. Taken together, 62 percent of people referred to treatment by the criminal justice system complete treatment or transfer to further treatment compared to 60 percent of people referred from other sources. People referred to treatment by the criminal justice system are more likely to end up incarcerated than people referred from other sources, 4 percent versus 1 percent, respectively.

This small difference in results does not justify the significant costs (including monetary, societal and personal) of justice system involvement such as participating in a drug court. This is particularly true when substantial barriers prevent low-income communities from accessing treatment that could have kept them out of the justice system in the first place.

Data from the Substance Abuse and Mental Health Services Administration shows that people living in poverty are more likely than people with more resources to need but not receive treatment. Of people living in poverty in 2006 and 2008 who needed substance abuse treatment, only about 18 percent received it. And people from this group with no health insurance coverage are more likely than those with insurance to need substance abuse treatment in the past year (14.9 percent versus 11.2 percent, respectively).

Public Safety Outcomes

While treatment in the community before someone is justice-involved is critical, policy makers and practitioners must still manage the reality that people are arrested for offenses related to an addiction. Drug courts are only one of a number of options available for addressing people with addictions who come into contact with the justice system.

Drug court advocates often cite their programs' low recidivism rates. But to understand real effectiveness, we must ask, "Compared to what?" Research shows that treatment works—it reduces the likelihood that someone will engage in future illegal activity and promotes positive life changes. However, treatment through the criminal justice system—and through drug courts—is not the only option, and some options may work better than others.

Recidivism rates are measured differently by each drug court program and the concurrent analyses of drug courts. Rearrest and reconviction rates are the most common measures, but an average reduction is hard to come by, as they can range from a 4 percent decrease in recidivism to a 70 [percent] decrease in some places.

The Washington State Institute for Public Policy frequently issues reports that examine the effectiveness of programs for people involved in the criminal and juvenile justice systems. In one report, researchers conducted a meta-analysis of 545 studies on programs working with people in the justice system—including 57 drug court studies—to determine which programs were the most effective in terms of reducing recidivism. They reported that adult drug courts could reduce recidivism rates by around 8.7 percent. Drug treatment in the community is quite comparable, reducing recidivism by 8.3 percent. In contrast, intensive supervision programs focused on treatment reduced crime by about 18 percent. Drug courts, therefore, do not necessarily have the best public safety outcomes of all justice-related treatment programs.

Problems with the Data

One of the challenges with studies that look at drug court outcomes is that it is difficult to have an appropriate control group. Control groups that are made up of non–drug court participants can be problematic because of underlying characteristics of people in that group, including possible reasons for their not being offered drug court (nature of their crime or addiction, criminal history, resources, etc.). In addition, with evidence of "cherry-picking" participants for drug courts, those who were admitted to the programs may already be more likely to succeed than their counterparts in the control groups.

Additionally, many of these studies are based on people who complete drug court—a variable fraction of those who

A Health-Centered Approach

A health-centered approach would ensure that drug use or the perceived need for treatment should *never be the reason* that people enter the criminal justice system, and that the criminal justice system should *never be the primary path* for people to receive such help. Individuals' drug problems can be addressed, families and communities preserved, public health and safety improved, and money saved by providing assistance to people not only after but also *before* drug use becomes problematic, *before* families fall apart, *before* disease spreads, *before* crimes are committed and *before* drug use becomes fatal.

"Drug Courts Are Not the Answer:
Toward a Health-Centered Approach to Drug Use,"
Drug Policy Alliance, March 22, 2011.
www.drugpolicy.org.

enter it—possibly making them more likely to succeed outside, as they have been able to follow the strict rules of a court for months and even years in some courts. Still, a number of studies that looked at longitudinal outcomes reaching to three years after participation in the drug court found little to no difference in recidivism rates for participants versus non-participants like people on probation; the Baltimore and Maricopa County drug courts showed little difference in rearrest rates, and participants in a Las Cruces, New Mexico, DWI (driving while intoxicated) court had similar traffic reconviction rates.

As drug courts continue to be one of the most expensive options for addressing the addiction issues of people in the justice system outside of prison, we should be putting the bulk of our resources where we get the most return.

Reforms Ignored in Favor of Drug Courts

Many studies about drug courts boast of their money-saving capabilities. However, drug courts carry hidden costs, including the lost opportunity to invest taxpayer dollars in ways that might be more effective. For example, drug court spending may reduce the amount available for other, non-justice strategies that, as outlined below, can provide a better return on investment.

At their inception, drug courts were meant to be an additional alternative to incarceration, not a way to avoid reforms in other areas of both the justice and public health systems. Over the last 20 years, drug courts have become a workaround and a distraction from making reforms in areas that could save jurisdictions money in the long run. Instead, drug courts draw scarce public dollars away from areas of reform such as:

- *Probation*: As the number of people under the supervision of the criminal justice system has increased, probation departments have increasingly been overwhelmed with large caseloads and reduced staffing. Rather than increasing funding for probation and the accompanying treatment services that are proven ways to help keep people in the community, criminal justice dollars are being directed toward drug courts, which can be more expensive per person and carry with them potentially harsher sanctions and requirements.

- *Treatment services in the community*: If less was spent on resource-intensive drug courts, treatment funding could increase to serve the already large numbers of people under justice supervision who need but do not receive treatment, and for those in the community who are currently not able to receive treatment due to inadequate funding of services for people with limited financial or insurance resources. Research presented in this report shows that treatment services are a far more cost-effective way of improving public safety, reducing the number of people in prison, and improving life outcomes.

• *Prevention and research*: While it is difficult to separate out spending by substance because people often use substances together, the National Center on Addiction and Substance Abuse at Columbia University estimated total government spending on drug use, excluding alcohol and tobacco, was estimated at around $18.7 billion in 2005—$16.4 billion in federal spending, $1.9 billion in state and $342 million in local health care spending. This includes $40 million in federal spending and $138 million in state spending on drug courts. Less than 2.5 percent of all substance abuse and addiction spending is for prevention, treatment, and research, which shows a focus on addressing the consequences of substance abuse rather than prevention and harm reduction.

Attention and funds directed at drug courts exemplify a continued reliance on the criminal justice system as a way to address a public health problem. Drug courts only reduce incarceration of and provide treatment to people *who already are in contact with the justice system*, doing nothing to help people avoid addiction-related criminal justice contact in the first place.

Reforms in these areas could drastically reduce the number of people in prison, while improving public safety and the health of communities. But to accomplish these reforms, public officials must prioritize funding for them; and in times of limited resources, this may mean reducing funding for drug courts.

The Total Cost of Drug Court

For people who would be prison bound if not for entering drug court, savings can be considerable—annual costs of sending one person to prison average $22,650, compared to an average of $4,300 per person for a year of drug court. If everyone who entered drug court was not given a jail sanction, successfully completed the drug court program, and went on to become a law-abiding resident, drug courts would be one of the most cost-effective means of working with people with drug problems who are involved in the criminal justice system. But this is not the case:

- Not everyone who is offered and accepts drug court would otherwise have gone to prison.

- In some courts, the average number of days spent in jail as sanctioned by the drug court judge can be as high as 50 or more, at an average cost of around $68 per day.

- Only a fraction of people who enter drug court will successfully complete it. From 33 to 75 percent of participants will be kicked out of drug court and be sentenced for the original offense, frequently more harshly than they would have if they had never attempted drug court.

Compounding the total cost of drug courts is that people who could have accessed treatment in the community or diversion program, for example, are potentially subject to the collateral consequences of a conviction. Some of the more prominent of these consequences include loss of food stamp benefits, decreased opportunities for student loans and employment, and denial of public housing, all of which increase the chances that a person will not be able to successfully stay out of prison in the future. In addition, sanctions for violating drug court rules, like failing drug tests, can send people to jail. Finally, failing to successfully complete the drug court program can mean a prison sentence, which in turn has been shown to be counterproductive to both individual recovery and improved public safety.

An Alternative to Drug Court

For those who do complete drug court, a number of studies have shown cost benefits, but not necessarily the most benefits per dollar when compared to alternatives. The Washington State Institute for Public Policy conducted a cost-benefit analysis of certain drug treatment programs, including drug courts, drug treatment in the community, and treatment in prison (either therapeutic community or outpatient). This analysis considered a number of studies to develop an average cost-benefit analysis, including a review of 57 studies on drug courts. They found that all three of these treatment types can reduce recidivism and are cost effective—that is, the benefits outweigh the costs. But drug treatment in the community was by far the most cost effective.

Researchers found that drug treatment in the community can reduce recidivism by 8.3 percent and produces $21 in benefits to victims and taxpayers in terms of reduced crime for every dollar spent. Drug treatment in prison produced only $7.74 in benefits, and drug courts less than $2 in benefits for every dollar spent. In other words, treatment in the community is about 10 times more cost effective than drug courts; it costs considerably less and is almost equally as effective as drug courts in reducing recidivism. In addition, treatment in the community allows people to stay with their families and contribute to their communities while also having more lifetime earnings—and therefore paying more taxes—than if they had received a conviction.

| "All Americans should be troubled by the extent to which incarceration has become a fixture in the life cycle of so many racial and ethnic minorities."

Racial Disparities in the Criminal Justice System Need to Be Addressed

Marc Mauer

In the following viewpoint, Marc Mauer argues that incarceration rates are disproportionately high in communities of color and that such unwarranted racial and ethnic disparities need to be reduced. Mauer contends that disproportionate crime rates only partially explain the incarceration rates of minorities and that racial profiling, discrimination against the poor, and criminal justice policies that are not race neutral need to be addressed in order to reduce disparities. Mauer is the executive director of the Sentencing Project, a national organization working for a fair and effective criminal justice system; he is the author of Race to Incarcerate.

Marc Mauer, "Justice for All? Challenging Racial Disparities in the Criminal Justice System," *Human Rights*, vol. 37, no. 4, Fall 2010, pp. 14–16. Copyright © 2010 by the American Bar Association. All rights reserved. Reproduced by permission.

As you read, consider the following questions:

1. Mauer claims that what percentage of the racial disparity in incarceration rates cannot be explained by differential offending patterns?

2. According to the author, in 2005 African Americans accounted for what percentage of persons sentenced to prison for a drug offense?

3. Mauer refers to a New Jersey state analysis finding that what percentage of persons serving prison time under the "school zone" drug law were African American or Latino?

There are many indicators of the profound impact of disproportionate rates of incarceration in communities of color. Perhaps the most stark among these are the data generated by the U.S. Department of Justice that project that if current trends continue, one of every three black males born today will go to prison in his lifetime, as will one of every six Latino males. (Rates of incarceration for women overall are lower than for men, but similar racial/ethnic disparities pertain.) Regardless of what one views as the causes of this situation, it should be deeply disturbing to all Americans that these figures represent the future for a generation of children growing up today.

This [viewpoint] will first present an overview of the factors that contribute to racial disparity in the justice system, and then it will recommend changes in policy and practice that could reduce these disparities without compromising public safety.

In order to develop policies and practices to reduce unwarranted racial disparities in the criminal justice system, it is necessary to assess the factors that have produced the current record levels of incarceration and racial/ethnic disparity. These are clearly complicated issues, but four areas of analysis are key:

- Disproportionate crime rates

- Disparities in criminal justice processing

- Overlap of race and class effects

- Impact of "race neutral" policies

Disproportionate Crime Rates

A series of studies conducted during the past thirty years has examined the degree to which disproportionate rates of incarceration for African Americans are related to greater involvement in crime. Examining national data for 1979, criminologist Alfred Blumstein concluded that 80 percent of racial disparity could be explained by greater involvement in crime, although a subsequent study reduced this figure to 76 percent for the 1991 prison population. But a similar analysis of 2004 imprisonment data by sentencing scholar Michael Tonry now finds that only 61 percent of the black incarceration rate is explained by disproportionate engagement in criminal behavior. Thus, nearly 40 percent of the racial disparity in incarceration today cannot be explained by differential offending patterns.

In addition, the national-level data may obscure variation among the states. A 1994 state-based assessment of these issues found broad variation in the extent to which higher crime rates among African Americans explained disproportionate imprisonment. Thus, while greater involvement in some crimes is related to higher rates of incarceration for African Americans, the weight of the evidence to date suggests that a significant proportion of the disparities is not a function of disproportionate criminal behavior.

Disparities in Criminal Justice Processing

Despite changes in leadership and growing attention to issues of racial and ethnic disparity in recent years, these disparities in criminal justice decision making still persist at every level of the criminal justice system. This does not necessarily suggest that these outcomes represent conscious efforts to discriminate, but they nonetheless contribute to excessive rates of imprisonment for some groups.

Disparities in processing have been seen most prominently in the area of law enforcement, with documentation of widespread racial profiling in recent years. National surveys conducted by the U.S. Department of Justice find that while African Americans may be subject to traffic stops by police at similar rates to whites, they are three times as likely to be searched after being stopped.

Disparate practices of law enforcement related to the "war on drugs" have been well documented in many jurisdictions and, in combination with sentencing policies, represent the most significant contributor to disproportionate rates of incarceration. This effect has come about through two overlapping trends. First, the escalation of the drug war has produced a remarkable rise in the number of people in prisons and jails either awaiting trial or serving time for a drug offense— increasing from 40,000 in 1980 to 500,000 today [in 2010]. Second, a general law enforcement emphasis on drug-related policing in communities of color has resulted in African Americans being prosecuted for drug offenses far out of proportion to the degree that they use or sell drugs. In 2005, African Americans represented 14 percent of current drug users, yet they constituted 33.9 percent of persons arrested for a drug offense and 53 percent of persons sentenced to prison for a drug offense.

Evidence of racial profiling by law enforcement does not suggest by any means that all agencies or all officers engage in such behaviors. In fact, in recent years, many police agencies have initiated training and oversight measures designed to prevent and identify such practices. Nevertheless, such behaviors still persist to some degree and clearly thwart efforts to promote racial justice.

Overlap of Race and Class Effects

Disparities in the criminal justice system are in part a function of the interrelationship between race and class and reflect the disadvantages faced by low-income defendants. This can be seen most prominently in regard to the quality of defense counsel. While many public defenders and appointed counsel provide high-quality legal support, in far too many jurisdictions the defense bar is characterized by high caseloads, poor training, and inadequate resources. In an assessment of this situation, the American Bar Association concluded that "too often the lawyers who provide defense services are inexperienced, fail to maintain adequate client contact, and furnish services that are simply not competent."

The limited availability of private resources disadvantages low-income people in other ways as well. For example, in considering whether a defendant will be released from jail prior to trial, owning a telephone is one factor used in making a recommendation so that the court can stay in contact with the defendant. But for persons who do not own a phone, this seemingly innocuous requirement becomes an obstacle to pretrial release.

At the sentencing stage, low-income substance abusers are also disadvantaged compared to defendants with resources. Given the general shortage of treatment programs, a defendant who has private insurance to cover the cost of treatment is in a much better position to make an argument for a non-incarcerative sentence than one who depends on publicly funded treatment programs.

Impact of "Race Neutral" Policies

Sentencing and related criminal justice policies that are ostensibly "race neutral" have in fact been seen over many years to have clear racial effects that could have been anticipated by legislators prior to enactment. Research on the development of punitive sentencing policies sheds light on the relationship between harsh sanctions and public perceptions of race. Criminologist Ted Chiricos and colleagues found that among whites, support for harsh sentencing policies was correlated with the degree to which a particular crime was perceived to be a "black" crime.

The federal crack cocaine sentencing laws of the 1980s have received significant attention due to their highly disproportionate racial outcomes, but other policies have produced similar effects. For example, a number of states and the federal government have adopted "school zone" drug laws that penalize drug offenses that take place within a certain distance of a school more harshly than other drug crimes.

The racial effect of these laws is an outgrowth of housing patterns. Because urban areas are more densely populated than suburban or rural areas, city residents are much more likely to be within a short distance of a school than are residents of suburban or rural areas. And because African Americans are more likely to live in urban neighborhoods than are whites, blacks convicted of a drug offense are subject to harsher penalties than whites committing a similar offense in a less-populated area. A state commission analysis of a "school zone" drug law in New Jersey, for example, documented that 96 percent of the persons serving prison time for such offenses were African American or Latino.

Recommendations for Policies and Practices

As indicated above, racial and ethnic disparities in the criminal justice system result from a complex set of policies and practices that may vary among jurisdictions. If we are committed to reducing unwarranted disparities in the system, it will require coordinated efforts among criminal justice leaders, policy makers, and community groups. Following are recommendations for initiatives that can begin to address these issues.

Shift the Focus of Drug Policies and Practice

State and federal policy makers should shift the focus of drug policies in ways that would be more effective in addressing substance abuse and would also reduce racial and ethnic disparities in incarceration. In broad terms, this should incorporate a shift in resources and focus to produce a more appropriate balance between law enforcement strategies and demand reduction approaches emphasizing prevention and treatment. Specific policy initiatives that would support these goals include enhancing public health models of community-based treatment that do not rely on the criminal justice system to provide services; identifying models of drug offender diversion in the court system that effectively target prison-bound defendants; repealing mandatory sentencing laws at the federal and state level to permit judges to impose sentences based on the specifics of the offender and the offense; and expanding substance abuse treatment options in prisons and providing sentence-reduction incentives for successful participation.

Provide Equal Access to Justice

Federal and state policy initiatives can aid in "leveling the playing field" by promoting equal access to justice. Such measures should incorporate adequate support for indigent defense services and provide a broader range and availability of community-based sentencing options.

These and similar initiatives clearly involve an expansion of resources in the court system and community. While these will impose additional short-term costs, they can be offset through appropriate reductions in the number and duration of prison sentences, long-term benefits of treatment and job placement services, and positive outcomes achieved by enhancing family and community stability.

Adopt Racial Impact Statements to Project Unanticipated Consequences of Criminal Justice Policies

Just as fiscal and environmental impact statements have become standard processes in many areas of public policy, so too can racial impact statements be used to assess the projected impact of new initiatives prior to their enactment. In 2008, Iowa and Connecticut each enacted such legislation, which calls for policy makers to receive an analysis of the anticipated effect of proposed sentencing legislation on the racial/ethnic composition of the state's prison population. If a disproportionate effect is projected, this does not preclude the legislative body from enacting the law if it is believed to be necessary for public safety, but it does provide an opportunity for discussion of racial disparities in such a way that alternative policies can be considered when appropriate.

A similar policy is currently in use in Minnesota, where the Sentencing Guidelines Commission regularly produces such analyses. Policies designed to produce racial impact statements should be adopted by legislative action or through the internal operations of a sentencing commission in all state and federal jurisdictions.

Assess the Racial Impact of Current Criminal Justice Decision Making

The Justice Integrity Act, first introduced in Congress in 2008, is designed to establish a process whereby any unwarranted disparities in federal prosecution can be analyzed and responded to when appropriate. Under the proposed bill, the attorney general would designate ten U.S. attorneys' offices as sites in which to set up task forces composed of representatives of the criminal justice system and the community. The task forces would be charged with reviewing and analyzing data on prosecutorial practices and developing initiatives designed to promote the twin goals of maintaining public safety and reducing disparity. Such a process would clearly be applicable to state justice systems as well.

While reasonable people may disagree about the causes of racial disparities in the criminal justice system, all Americans should be troubled by the extent to which incarceration has become a fixture in the life cycle of so many racial and ethnic minorities. The impact of such dramatic rates of imprisonment has profound consequences for children growing up in these neighborhoods, mounting fiscal burdens, and reductions in public support for vital services.

These developments also contribute to eroding trust in the justice system in communities of color—an outcome that is clearly counterproductive to public safety goals. It is long past time for the nation to commit itself to a comprehensive assessment of the causes and remedies for addressing these issues.

> *"Black offenders do not receive stiffer penalties than white offenders for equivalent crimes—not today, and not at any time in recent decades."*

There Is No Evidence of Racial Discrimination in the Criminal Justice System

John Perazzo

In the following viewpoint, John Perazzo argues that President Barack Obama was wrong to claim that there is racism in the criminal justice system. Perazzo contends that the overrepresentation of blacks in the justice system is the result of higher crime rates, not of discrimination. Perazzo claims that several decades of criminal justice literature supports the conclusion that there is no evidence of racial discrimination in the arrest, trial, or sentencing of criminal defendants. Perazzo is the managing editor of Discover the Networks, *a database of the political Left, and he is the author of* The Myths That Divide Us: How Lies Have Poisoned American Race Relations.

As you read, consider the following questions:

1. Perazzo claims that black overrepresentation in the criminal justice system is almost entirely at what stage?

2. The author claims that in a 1996 analysis of felony cases, blacks were convicted at a lower rate than whites in how many of the fourteen felony categories?

3. According to Perazzo, drug possession accounts for what percentage of offenses that land people in federal prisons?

In an interview published December 10th [2008] in the *Chicago Tribune* and the *Los Angeles Times*, Barack Obama stated that one of his top priorities as president will be to put an end to racial discrimination in the criminal justice system. This pledge is consistent with his oft-repeated campaign promise to "eliminate disparities in criminal sentencing," most notably "the disparity between sentencing [for] crack and powder-based cocaine," which Obama said was "wrong and should be completely eliminated." At a presidential primary debate in January 2008, Obama asserted that blacks and whites "are arrested at very different rates, are convicted at very different rates, [and] receive very different sentences . . . for the same crime." On another occasion he sounded a similar theme: "We have certain sentences that are based less on the kind of crime you commit than on what you look like and where you come from." Though neither the media nor the [2008 Republican presidential candidate John] McCain campaign dared to challenge any of Obama's presumably sacrosanct pronouncements about racism in the justice system, the fact remains that every one of those pronouncements was an unadulterated falsehood.

The Overrepresentation of Blacks

Long ago, the injustices which Obama references certainly existed, particularly in the South. But it hardly seems appropriate for a supposedly forward-looking president—who founded his entire campaign on a platform of "change"—to continue fighting yesteryear's battles again and again. Simply put, black offenders do not receive stiffer penalties than white offenders for equivalent crimes—not today, and not at any time in recent decades. The most exhaustive, best designed study of this matter—a three-year analysis of more than 11,000 convicted criminals in California—found that the severity of offenders' sentences depended heavily on such factors as prior criminal records, the seriousness of the crimes, and whether guns were used in the commission of those crimes. Race was found to have no effect whatsoever. In fact the researcher, Joan Petersilia, was forced to admit that these results contradicted conclusions she had drawn from an earlier study—in which she had not taken prior convictions and the use of firearms into account.

The criminal justice process is composed of a number of stages, or decision points, at which law enforcement personnel such as police and judges must decide how to proceed (i.e., whether to make an arrest, whether to convict or acquit a defendant, or whether to impose a harsh or a mild sentence). Contrary to popular mythology, there is no evidence of racial discrimination at any of these decision points. Black overrepresentation is almost entirely at the arrest stage—reflecting the simple fact that the "average" black breaks the law more frequently than the "average" white. The National Crime Victimization Surveys . . . show that statistically the "average" black is far more likely than the "average" white to be identified, by a victim or witness, as the perpetrator of a violent crime. This racial gap, moreover, is approximately equal to the racial gap in actual arrest rates. "As long ago as 1978," says Manhattan Institute scholar Heather Mac Donald, "a study of robbery and aggravated assault in eight cities found parity between the race of assailants in victim identifications and in arrests—a finding replicated many times since, across a range of crimes."

At all the decision points subsequent to arrest, the outcomes are virtually identical for blacks and whites alike—and the slight differences that do exist tend to favor blacks. In

The High Incarceration Rate of Blacks

The favorite culprits for high black prison rates include a biased legal system, draconian drug enforcement and even prison itself. None of these explanations stands up to scrutiny.

The black incarceration rate is overwhelmingly a function of black crime. Insisting otherwise only worsens black alienation and further defers a real solution to the black crime problem.

Heather Mac Donald,
"High Incarceration Rate of Blacks Is Function of Crime,
Not Racism," Investor's Business Daily, April 28, 2008.

studies that consider all relevant variables—such as the defendant's prior criminal record, the severity of the crime in question, the offender's demeanor with police, whether a weapon was used, and whether the crime in question was victim precipitated—no differences have been found in sentencing patterns, either in relation to the victim's race or the offender's race.

The Criminal Justice Literature

In 1983, the liberal-leaning National Academy of Sciences found "no evidence of a widespread systematic pattern of discrimination in sentencing." In 1985, the *Journal of Criminal Law and Criminology* concluded that a disproportionate number of blacks were in prison not because of a double standard of justice, but because of the disproportionate number of crimes they committed. That same year, federal government statistician Patrick Langan conducted an exhaustive study of black and white incarceration rates and found that "even if racism [in sentencing] exists, it might help explain only a small part of the gap between the 11 percent black representation in the United States' adult population and the now nearly 50 percent black representation among persons entering state prisons each year in the United States." In a 1987 review essay of the three most comprehensive books examining the role of race in the American criminal justice system, the journal *Criminology* concluded that there was little evidence of anti-black discrimination. A 1991 RAND Corporation study found that a defendant's racial or ethnic group affiliation bore little or no relationship to conviction rates; far more important than race were such factors as the amount of evidence against the defendant, and whether or not a credible eyewitness testified. This same study found almost no relation between a defendant's race or ethnicity and his or her likelihood of receiving a severe sentence. A 1993 study by the National Academy of Sciences agreed that race had a negligible effect on sentencing. Also in 1993, a study of federal sentencing guidelines found no evidence of racially disparate punishments for perpetrators of similar offenses. The seriousness of the crime, the offender's prior criminal record, and whether weapons were used accounted for all the observed interracial variations of prison sentences.

In 1995, Patrick Langan analyzed data on 42,500 defendants in America's 75 largest counties and found "no evidence that in the places where blacks in the United States have most of their contacts with the justice system, that system treats them more harshly than whites." A 1996 analysis of 55,000 big-city felony cases found that black defendants were convicted at a lower rate than whites in 12 of the 14 federally designated felony categories. This finding is consistent with the overwhelming consensus of other recent studies, most of which indicate that black defendants are slightly less likely to be convicted of criminal charges against them than white defendants. Liberal criminologist Michael Tonry wrote in his

1996 book *Malign Neglect*: "Racial differences in patterns of offending, not racial bias by police and other officials, are the principal reason that such greater proportions of blacks than whites are arrested, prosecuted, convicted and imprisoned." The following year, liberal criminologists Robert Sampson and Janet Lauritsen concurred that "large racial differences in criminal offending," not racism, accounted for the fact that blacks were likelier than whites to be in prison and serving longer terms.

In short, notwithstanding Barack Obama's professed concerns about "discrimination" in the justice system, it is entirely demonstrable that even two and three decades ago charges of racial inequities were largely chimeras [fabrications of the mind] without basis in objective reality. Nothing in the criminal justice literature of the past decade indicates that anything has changed in that regard.

The Difference in Drug Penalties

As noted above, president-elect Obama has complained that the penalties for possession of crack cocaine, a drug most often used by poor blacks, are much harsher than the penalties for possession of powder cocaine, whose users are typically affluent whites. The implication is that the imposition of harsh anti-crack penalties was rooted, at least initially, in racism. But the *Congressional Record* shows that such was not at all the case. In 1986, when the strict, federal anti-crack legislation was being debated, the Congressional Black Caucus (CBC)— deeply concerned about the degree to which crack was decimating black communities—strongly supported the legislation and actually pressed for even harsher penalties. In fact, a few years earlier CBC members had pushed President [Ronald] Reagan to create the Office of National Drug Control Policy.

Incidentally, Obama fails to mention that the vast majority of cocaine arrests in the U.S. are made at the state—not the federal—level, where sentencing disparities between cases involving crack and powder cocaine generally do not exist; indeed, only 13 states punish crack convictions more harshly than powder convictions, and the differentials are much smaller than those on the federal level. Furthermore, drug possession accounts for fewer than 2 percent of all offenses that propel individuals into federal prisons. Those most likely to be incarcerated for drug convictions are not mere users, but traffickers who are largely career criminals with very long rap sheets. [Editor's note: Federal sentencing disparities were eliminated by Congress in 2010.]

Moreover, it is reasonable to wonder why Obama feels compelled to speak out about alleged inequities vis-à-vis federal cocaine penalties (which he says discriminate against blacks), but is silent on the matter of federal methamphetamine-trafficking penalties—which, it could easily be argued, discriminate heavily against whites. Heather Mac Donald explains:

> The press almost never mentions the federal methamphetamine-trafficking penalties, which are identical to those for crack: five grams of meth net you a mandatory minimum five-year sentence. In 2006, the 5,391 sentenced federal meth defendants (nearly as many as the [5,619] crack defendants) were 54 percent white, 39 percent Hispanic, and 2 percent black. But no one calls the federal meth laws anti-Hispanic or anti-white.

In the final analysis, Barack Obama's assertions about inequities in the justice system ring absolutely hollow today, just as they have rung hollow for at least a quarter century. To be sure, it is possible that the president-elect is ignorant of the facts presented herein and, as such, is simply parroting the misinformation to which he has been exposed. Another possibility is that Obama is entirely aware of the actual facts but has elected instead to play the time-honored political game of fabricating pernicious "injustices" that allegedly plague an entire demographic of "victims"—and then positioning himself as the hero who will save the day. Neither of those two scenarios casts the president-elect in a dignified light.

Periodical and Internet Sources Bibliography

The following articles have been selected to supplement the diverse views presented in this chapter.

Radley Balko	"Wrongful Convictions," *Reason*, July 2011.
Ellis Cose	"A New Jim Crow?," *Newsweek*, January 27, 2010.
Drug Policy Alliance	"Drug Courts Are Not the Answer: Toward a Health-Centered Approach to Drug Use," March 22, 2011. www.drugpolicy.org.
Sunil Dutta	"How to Fix America's Broken Criminal Justice System," *Christian Science Monitor*, December 30, 2010.
Nicole A. Gaines	"Discrimination Is the Well-Documented Cause of Race Disparity in Prison," *Seattle Times*, October 29, 2010.
John Wesley Hall	"A Fairer and More Democratic Federal Grand Jury System," *Federal Sentencing Register*, June 2008.
Marc Levin	"Cutting Crime. Cutting Costs. Reinforcing Conservatism," Townhall.com, February 11, 2011.
Dahlia Lithwick	"A Separate Peace," *Newsweek*, February 10, 2010.
National Association of Criminal Defense Lawyers	"America's Problem-Solving Courts: The Criminal Costs of Treatment and the Case for Reform," September 2009. www.nacdl.org.
Tracy Veláquez	"The Verdict on Drug Courts," *Nation*, December 27, 2010.

OPPOSING
VIEWPOINTS®
SERIES

CHAPTER 2

What Is the State of the Incarceration System in the United States?

Chapter Preface

According to the US Bureau of Justice Statistics, in 2010 there were approximately 1.6 million people in prison and approximately 750,000 people in local jails, making the ratio of imprisoned adults in America about one in one hundred. An additional five million people were on probation or parole, bringing the total number of Americans under correctional supervision to more than 7.3 million—more than 3 percent of the adult population. The cost of retaining this number of individuals under correctional supervision has also grown. A 2009 report by the Pew Center on the States' Public Safety Performance Project states that in fiscal year 2008, state corrections spending topped $51 billion and federal spending for corrections was $900 million. With state budgets increasingly strapped for cash, the high spending on incarceration has come under the microscope.

The report goes on to explain that of state corrections spending, 88 percent goes to prisons and the rest to probation and parole. Although prison cost varies among states, in 2009 the average cost per prisoner per year was $29,000, based on thirty-three surveyed states. By contrast, the average annual cost for probation was only $1,250 and for parole—supervision of inmates who are released from prison to serve the rest of their sentence under supervision on the outside—only $2,750.

The cost concerns have caused several state governors and legislatures to change their approach to incarceration, in some cases even closing prisons. Governor Andrew M. Cuomo of New York State announced in mid-2011 that seven New York prisons would be closed. Cuomo was facing a $10 billion budget gap and closing prisons was part of the solution, saving what he anticipated would amount to $184 million over the first two years after closing. In a 2011 statement, Cuomo said,

"The state's prison system has been too inefficient and too costly, with far more capacity than what is needed to secure the state's inmate population and ensure the public's safety." Given that the state's prison population had dropped, the prisons were deemed an unnecessary expense.

The high population of inmates in American prisons results in high costs for taxpayers. Especially given the tough economic times following the recession of the late 2000s and early 2010s, that spending must be justified as effective and necessary in order to continue. The authors in the following chapter debate the effectiveness of the higher levels of incarceration and consider alternatives to prisons.

| "At the deepest level, many of these shifts, taken together, suggest that crime in the United States is falling . . . because of a big improvement in the culture."

Greater Incarceration and a Change in Culture Explain the Decline in Crime

James Q. Wilson

In the following viewpoint, James Q. Wilson argues that other factors besides unemployment and poverty explain crime rates. Wilson contends that a recent decline in crime is not due to economic factors but rather is the result of imprisonment, policing, less lead in the environment, and less cocaine abuse. In particular, he notes that the crime rate among blacks has fallen dramatically. Wilson concludes that the overarching explanation for the falling crime rate is an improvement in American culture. Wilson is a professor and senior fellow at the Clough Center for the Study of Constitutional Democracy at Boston College.

As you read, consider the following questions:

1. According to Wilson, by what percentage did the unemployment rate increase in the recent recession?

James Q. Wilson, "Crime and the Great Recession," *City Journal*, vol. 21, no. 3, Summer 2011. Reproduced by permission.

2. By what fraction did the amount of lead in Americans' blood fall between 1975 and 1991, according to the author?

3. Wilson contends that whereas in 1980 arrests of young blacks outnumbered arrests of young whites by more than six to one, by 2002 the ratio fell to what?

During the seventies and eighties, scarcely any newspaper story about rising crime failed to mention that it was strongly linked to unemployment and poverty. The argument was straightforward: If less legitimate work was available, more illegal work would take place. Certain scholars agreed. Economist Gary [S.] Becker of the University of Chicago, a Nobel laureate, developed a powerful theory that crime was rational—that a person will commit crime if the expected utility exceeds that of using his time and other resources in pursuit of alternative activities, such as leisure or legitimate work. Observation may appear to bear this theory out; after all, neighborhoods with elevated crime rates tend to be those where poverty and unemployment are high as well.

Unemployment and Crime

But the notion that unemployment causes crime runs into some obvious difficulties. For one thing, the 1960s, a period of rising crime, had essentially the same unemployment rate as the late 1990s and early 2000s, a period when crime fell. Further, during the Great Depression, when unemployment hit 25 percent, the crime rate in many cities went down. (True, national crime statistics weren't very useful back in the 1930s, but studies of local police records and individual citizens by scholars such as Glen Elder have generally found reduced crime, too.) Among the explanations offered for this puzzle is that unemployment and poverty were so common during the Great Depression that families became closer, devoted themselves to mutual support, and kept young people, who might be more inclined to criminal behavior, under constant adult supervision. These days, because many families are weaker and children are more independent, we would not see the same effect, so certain criminologists continue to suggest that a 1 percent increase in the unemployment rate should produce as much as a 2 percent increase in property crime rates.

Yet when the recent [in the late 2000s] recession struck, that didn't happen. As the national unemployment rate doubled from around 5 percent to nearly 10 percent, the property crime rate, far from spiking, fell significantly. For 2009, the FBI [Federal Bureau of Investigation] reported an 8 percent drop in the nationwide robbery rate and a 17 percent reduction in the auto theft rate from the previous year. Big-city reports show the same thing. Between 2008 and 2010, New York City experienced a 4 percent decline in the robbery rate and a 10 percent fall in the burglary rate. Boston, Chicago, and Los Angeles witnessed similar declines. The FBI's latest numbers, for 2010, show that the national crime rate fell again.

Some scholars argue that the unemployment rate is too crude a measure of economic frustration to prove the connection between unemployment and crime, since it estimates only the percentage of the labor force that is looking for work and hasn't found it. But other economic indicators tell much the same story. The labor-force participation rate lets us determine the percentage of the labor force that is neither working nor looking for work—individuals who are, in effect, detached from the labor force. These people should be especially vulnerable to criminal inclinations, if the bad-economy-leads-to-crime theory holds. In 2008, though, even as crime was falling, only about half of men aged 16 to 24 (who are disproportionately likely to commit crimes) were in the labor force, down from over two-thirds in 1988, and a comparable decline took place among African American men (who are also disproportionately likely to commit crimes).

The University of Michigan's Consumer Sentiment Index offers another way to assess the link between the economy and crime. This measure rests on thousands of interviews asking people how their financial situations have changed over the last year, how they think the economy will do during the next year, and about their plans for buying durable goods. The index measures the way people *feel*, rather than the objective conditions they face. It has proved a very good predictor of stock market behavior and, for a while, of the crime rate, which tended to climb when people lost confidence. When the index collapsed in 2009 and 2010, the stock market predictably went down with it—but this time, the crime rate went down, too.

The Impact of Imprisonment

So we have little reason to ascribe the recent crime decline to jobs, the labor market, or consumer sentiment. The question remains: Why is crime falling?

One obvious answer is that many more people are in prison than in the past. Experts differ on the size of the effect, but I think that William Spelman and Steven Levitt have it right in believing that greater incarceration can explain one-quarter or more of the crime decline. Yes, many thoughtful observers think that we put too many offenders in prison for too long. For some criminals, such as low-level drug dealers and former inmates returned to prison for parole violations, that may be so. But it's true nevertheless that when prisoners are kept off the street, they can attack only one another, not you or your family.

Imprisonment's crime-reduction effect helps explain why the burglary, car theft, and robbery rates are lower in the United States than in England. The difference results not from willingness to send convicted offenders to prison, which is about the same in both countries, but in how long America keeps them behind bars. For the same offense, you will spend more time in prison here than in England. Still, prison can't be the sole reason for the recent crime drop in this country: Canada has seen roughly the same decline in crime, but its imprisonment rate has been relatively flat for at least two decades.

Another possible reason for reduced crime is that potential victims may have become better at protecting themselves by equipping their homes with burglar alarms, installing extra locks on their cars, and moving into safer buildings or even safer neighborhoods. We have only the faintest idea, however, about how common these trends are or what effects on crime they may have.

A Change in Policing

Policing, as *City Journal* readers know, has become more disciplined over the last two decades; these days, it tends to be driven by the desire to reduce crime, rather than simply to maximize arrests, and that shift has reduced crime rates. One of the most important innovations is what has been called hot-spot policing. The great majority of crimes tend to occur in the same places. Put active police resources in those areas instead of telling officers to drive around waiting for 911 calls, and you can bring down crime. The hot-spot idea helped make the New York [City] Police Department's Compstat program—its planning and accountability system, which, using computerized maps, pinpoints where crime is taking place and enables police chiefs to hold precinct captains responsible for targeting those areas—so effective.

Researchers continue to test and refine hot-spot policing. For instance, criminologists Lawrence Sherman and David Weisburd, after analyzing data from more than 7,000 police arrivals at various locations in Minneapolis, showed that for every minute that an officer spent at a spot, the length of time without a crime there after the officer departed went up—until the officer had been gone for over 15 minutes. After that

Violent vs. Nonviolent Crimes

Imprisonment is the right policy for anyone committing heinous crimes like rape, assaults, robbery at gunpoint, and many other crimes where victims are badly harmed both physically and mentally. Imprisonment is the wrong punishment for crimes without victims, or where other punishments are more effective.

Gary Becker,
"Does America Imprison Too Many People?,"
The Becker-Posner Blog, December 4, 2011.
www.becker-posner-blog.com.

gap, the crime rate went up. The police can make the best use of their time by staying at a hot spot for a while, moving on, and returning after 15 minutes have elapsed.

Some cities now use a computer-based system for mapping traffic accidents and crime rates. They have noticed that the two measures tend to coincide: Where there are more accidents, there is more crime. In Shawnee, Kansas, the police spent a lot more time in about 4 percent of the city's area where one-third of the crime occurred: Burglaries then fell in that area by 60 percent (even though in the city as a whole, they fell by only 8 percent), and traffic accidents went down by 17 percent.

Substances That Increase Crime

There may also be a medical reason for the crime decline. For decades, doctors have known that children with lots of lead in their blood are much more likely to be aggressive, violent, and delinquent. In 1974, the Environmental Protection Agency required oil companies to stop putting lead in gasoline. At the same time, lead in paint was banned for any new home (though old buildings still have lead paint, which children can absorb). Tests have shown that the amount of lead in Americans' blood fell by four-fifths between 1975 and 1991. A 2000 study by economist Rick Nevin suggested that the reduction in gasoline lead produced more than half of the decline in violent crime during the nineties. A later study by Nevin claimed that this also happened in other nations. Another economist, Jessica Wolpaw Reyes, has made the same argument. (One oddity about this fascinating claim has yet to be explained: why the reduction related to lead-free blood included only violent crime, not property offenses.)

Yet one more shift that has probably helped bring down crime is the decrease in heavy cocaine use in many states. Measuring cocaine use is no easy matter; one has to infer it from interviews or from hospital admission rates. Between 1992 and 2009, the number of admissions for cocaine or crack use fell by nearly two-thirds. In 1999, 9.8 percent of 12th-grade students said that they had tried cocaine; by 2010, that figure had fallen to 5.5 percent.

What we really need to know, though, is not how many people tried coke but how many are heavy users. Casual users who regard coke as a party drug are probably less likely to commit serious crimes than heavier users who may resort to theft and violence to feed their craving. But a study by Jonathan Caulkins at Carnegie Mellon University found that the total demand for cocaine dropped between 1988 and 2010, with a sharp decline among both light and heavy users. This fall in demand may help explain why cocaine has become cheaper, despite intense law enforcement efforts aimed at disrupting its distribution. Illegal markets, like legal ones, cut prices when demand falls.

A Reduction in Crimes
Committed by Blacks

Blacks still constitute the core of America's crime problem. But the African American crime rate, too, has been falling, probably because of the same noneconomic factors behind falling crime in general: imprisonment, policing, environmental changes, and less cocaine abuse.

Knowing the exact crime rate of any ethnic or racial group isn't easy, since most crimes don't result in arrest or conviction, and those that do may be an unrepresentative fraction of all crimes. Nevertheless, we do know the racial characteristics of those who *have* been arrested for crimes, and they show that the number of blacks arrested has been falling. Barry Latzer of the John Jay College of Criminal Justice has demonstrated that between 1980 and 2005, arrests of blacks for homicide and other violent crimes fell by about half nationwide.

It's also suggestive that in the five New York City precincts where the population is at least 80 percent black, the murder rate fell by 78 percent between 1990 and 2000. In the black neighborhoods of Chicago, which remains a higher-crime city than New York, burglary fell by 52 percent, robbery by 62 percent, and homicide by 33 percent between 1991 and 2003. A skeptic might retort that all these seeming gains were merely the result of police officers' giving up and no longer recording crimes in black neighborhoods. But the skeptic would have a hard time explaining why opinion surveys in Chicago show that, among blacks, fear of crime was cut in half during the same period.

One can cite further evidence of a turnaround in black crime. Researchers at the federal Office of Juvenile Justice and Delinquency Prevention found that in 1980, arrests of young blacks outnumbered arrests of whites by more than six to one. By 2002, the gap had been closed to just under four to one.

Drug use among blacks has changed even more dramatically than it has among the population as a whole. As Latzer points out—and his argument is confirmed by a study by Bruce D. Johnson, Andrew Golub, and Eloise Dunlap—among 13,000 people arrested in Manhattan between 1987 and 1997, a disproportionate number of whom were black, those born between 1948 and 1969 were heavily involved with crack co-caine, but those born after 1969 used little crack and instead smoked marijuana. The reason was simple: The younger African Americans had known many people who used crack and other hard drugs and wound up in prisons, hospitals, and morgues. The risks of using marijuana were far less serious. This shift in drug use, if the New York City experience is borne out in other locations, can help explain the fall in black inner-city crime rates after the early 1990s.

John Donohue and Steven Levitt have advanced an additional explanation for the reduction in black crime: the legalization of abortion, which resulted in black children's never being born into circumstances that would have made them likelier to become criminals. I have ignored that explanation because it remains a strongly contested finding, challenged by two economists at the Federal Reserve Bank of Boston and by various academics.

An Improvement in the Culture

At the deepest level, many of these shifts, taken together, suggest that crime in the United States is falling—even through the greatest economic downturn since the Great Depression—because of a big improvement in the culture. The cultural argument may strike some as vague, but writers have relied on it in the past to explain both the Great Depression's fall in crime and the sixties' crime explosion. In the first period, on this view, people took self-control seriously; in the second, self-expression—at society's cost—became more prevalent. It is a plausible case.

Culture creates a problem for social scientists like me, however. We do not know how to study it in a way that produces hard numbers and tested theories. Culture is the realm of novelists and biographers, not of data-driven social scientists. But we can take some comfort, perhaps, in reflecting that identifying the likely causes of the crime decline is even more important than precisely measuring it.

| "The failure of the great experiment in mass incarceration is rooted in three fallacies of the tough-on-crime perspective."

The Benefits of Mass Incarceration Are Outweighed by the Negative Effects

Bruce Western

In the following viewpoint, Bruce Western argues that the dramatic increase in the incarceration rate over the last few decades has resulted in only a modest decrease in crime while causing new problems. Western claims that mass imprisonment has harmed prisoners, their families, and their social groups. He contends that the money spent on incarceration is poorly spent and that the policy of mass incarceration rests on misguided views about criminality. Western is a professor of sociology and director of the Malcolm Wiener Center for Social Policy at Harvard University. He is the author of Punishment and Inequality in America.

As you read, consider the following questions:

1. According to Western, how many people are in US prisons and jails?

Bruce Western, "Reentry: Reversing Mass Imprisonment," *Boston Review*, vol. 33, no. 4, July/August 2008. Copyright © 2008 by Bruce Western. All rights reserved. Reproduced by permission.

2. How much money was spent in additional correctional spending from 1993 to 2001 to pay for half a million new prison inmates, according to the author?

3. Western claims that money spent on prison construction was diverted from what two programs that could have benefited the poor?

The British sociologist T.H. Marshall described citizenship as the "basic human equality associated with full membership in a community." By this measure, thirty years of prison growth concentrated among the poorest in society has diminished American citizenship. But as the prison boom attains new heights, the conversation about criminal punishment may finally be shifting.

The American Prison Boom

For the first time in decades, political leaders seem willing to consider the toll of rising incarceration rates. In October last year [2007], Senator Jim Webb convened hearings of the Joint Economic Committee on the social costs of mass incarceration. In opening the hearings, Senator Webb made a remarkable observation, "With the world's largest prison population," he said, "our prisons test the limits of our democracy and push the boundaries of our moral identity." Like T.H. Marshall, Webb recognized that our political compact is based on a fundamental equality among citizens. Deep inequalities stretch the bonds of citizenship and ultimately imperil the quality of democracy. Extraordinary in the current political climate, Webb inquired into the prison's significance, not just for crime, but also for social inequality. The incarceration bubble has not burst yet, but Webb's hearings are one signal of a welcome thaw in tough-on-crime politics.

There are now 2.3 million people in U.S. prisons and jails, a fourfold increase in the incarceration rate since 1980. During the fifty years preceding our current three-decade surge, the scale of imprisonment was largely unchanged. And the impact of this rise has hardly been felt equally in society; the American prison boom is as much a story about race and class as it is about crime control. Nothing separates the social experience of blacks and whites like involvement in the criminal justice system. Blacks are seven times more likely to be incarcerated than whites, and large racial disparities can be seen for all age groups and at different levels of education. One in nine black men in their twenties is now in prison or jail. Young black men today are more likely to do time in prison than serve in the military or graduate college with a bachelor's degree. The large black-white disparity in incarceration is unmatched by most other social indicators. Racial disparities in unemployment (two to one), nonmarital childbearing (three to one), infant mortality (two to one), and wealth (one to five) are all significantly lower than the seven to one black-white ratio in incarceration rates.

Though lurid portrayals of black criminality are easy to find on the local news or reality TV, the deep class divisions in imprisonment may be less apparent. Nearly all the growth in imprisonment since 1980 has been concentrated among those with no more than a high school education. Among young black men who have never been to college, one in five is incarcerated, and one in three will go to prison at some time in their lives. The intimate link between school failure and incarceration is clear at the bottom of the education ladder where 60 percent of black, male high school dropouts will go to prison before age thirty-five. The stigma of official criminality has become normal for these poorly educated black men, and they are thereby converted from merely disadvantaged into a class of social outsiders. These astonishing levels of punishment are new. We need only go back two decades to find a time when imprisonment was not a common event in the lives of black men with less than a college education.

The Effects of Incarceration

The effects of prison are not confined within its walls. Those coming home from prison, now about 700,000 each year, face a narrowed array of life chances. Mostly returning to urban neighborhoods of concentrated poverty, men with prison records are often out of work. The jobs they do find pay little and offer only a fraction of the earnings growth that usually supports the socially valuable roles of husband and breadwinner. Ex-prisoners are often in poor health, sometimes struggling with mental illness or chronic disease. A University of California, Berkeley study attributes most of the black-white difference in AIDS infection to racial disparities in incarceration. In many cases, people with felony records are denied housing, education, and welfare benefits. In eleven states, they are permanently denied the right to vote.

The social penalties of imprisonment also spread through families. Though formerly incarcerated men are just as likely to have children as other men of the same age, they are less likely to get married. Those who are married will most likely divorce or separate. The family instability surrounding incarceration persists across generations. Among children born since 1990, 4 percent of whites and 25 percent of blacks will witness their father being sent to prison by their fourteenth birthday. Those children, too, are to some extent drawn into the prison nexus, riding the bus to far-flung correctional facilities and passing through metal detectors and pat-downs on visiting day. In short, those with prison records and their families are something less than full members of society. To be young, black, and unschooled today is to risk a felony conviction, prison time, and a life of second-class citizenship. In this sense, the prison boom has produced mass incarceration—a level of imprisonment so vast and concentrated that it forges the collective experience of an entire social group.

Viewed in historical context, mass incarceration takes on even greater significance. The prison boom took off in the

Children Are Affected by High Incarceration Rates

It isn't just offenders whose lives are damaged. . . . 54 percent of inmates are parents with minor children, including more than 120,000 mothers and 1.1 million fathers. One in every 28 children has a parent incarcerated, up from 1 in 125 just 25 years ago. Two-thirds of these children's parents were incarcerated for nonviolent offenses.

Veronique de Rugy, "Prison Math," Reason, July 2011.

1970s, immediately following the great gains to citizenship hard won by the civil rights movement. Growing rates of incarceration mean that, in the experience of African Americans in poor neighborhoods, the advancement of voting rights, school desegregation, and protection from discrimination was substantially halted. Mass incarceration undermined the project for full African American citizenship and revealed the obstacles to political equality presented by acute social disparity.

The Reduction in Crime

Skeptics may concede that mass incarceration injured social justice, but surely, they would contend, it contributed to the tremendous decline in crime through the 1990s. Indeed, the crime decline of the '90s produced a great improvement in public safety. From 1993 to 2001, the violent crime rate fell considerably, murder rates in big cities like New York and Los Angeles dropped by half or more, and this progress in social well-being was recorded by rich and poor alike. Yet, when I analyzed crime rates in this period, I found that rising prison populations did not reduce crime by much. The growth in state imprisonment accounted for 2–5 percent of the decline in serious crime—one-tenth of the crime drop from 1993 to 2001. The remaining nine-tenths was due to factors like the increasing size of local police forces, the pacification of the drug trade following the crack epidemic of the early 1990s, and the role of local circumstances that resist a general explanation.

So a modest decline in serious crime over an eight-year period was purchased for $53 billion in additional correctional spending and half a million new prison inmates: a large price to pay for a small reduction. If we add the lost earnings of prisoners to the family disruption and community instability produced by mass incarceration, we cannot help but acknowledge that a steep price was paid for a small improvement in public safety. Several examples further demonstrate that the boom may have been a waste because crime can be controlled without large increases in imprisonment. Violent crime in Canada, for example, also declined greatly through the 1990s, but Canadian incarceration rates actually fell from 1991 to 1999. New York maintained particularly low crime rates through the 2000s, but has been one of the few states to cut its prison population in recent years.

More importantly, perhaps, the reduction in crime was accompanied by an array of new problems associated with mass incarceration. Those states that have sought reduced crime through mass incarceration find themselves faced with an array of problems associated with overreliance on imprisonment. How can poor communities with few resources absorb the return of 700,000 prisoners each year? How can states pay for their prisons while responding to the competing demands of higher education, Medicaid, and K–12 schools? How can we address the social costs—the broken homes, unemployment, and crime—that can follow from imprisonment? Questions such as these lead us to a more fundamental concern: How can mass imprisonment be reversed and American citizenship repaired?

The Origins of Mass Incarceration

We can begin to tackle these issues by understanding how we got here. The origins of today's mass incarceration can be traced to basic political and economic shifts in the 1960s. On the economic side, the prison population swelled following the collapse of the urban manufacturing industry and subsequent cascade of social ills that swept poor inner-city neighborhoods. Serious crime—the traditional target of the penal system—was an important part of these urban social problems. Murder rates in large cities grew dramatically from 1965 to 1980. But in addition to the problem of serious crime, the penal system was used to manage many of the by-products of persistent poverty: untreated drug addiction and mental illness, homelessness, chronic idleness among young men, and social disorder. It was the management of these social problems, not serious crime, that fueled incarceration rates for drug users, public-order offenders, and parole violators.

As the social crisis of urban America supplied the masses for mass incarceration, the penal system itself became more punitive. The tough-on-crime message honed by the Republican Party in national politics since the [Barry] Goldwater campaign of 1964 spoke to the racial anxieties of white voters discomfited by civil rights protests and summertime waves of civil unrest felt in cities through the decade. Conservatives charged that liberals coddled criminals and excused crime with phony root causes like poverty and unemployment. President [Richard] Nixon launched a war on crime, only to be surpassed by President [Ronald] Reagan's war on drugs, which applied the resources of federal law enforcement to the problem of drug control. Policy experts abandoned rehabilitation, concluding that prisons could only deter and warehouse those who would otherwise commit crime in society. These politics produced a revolution in criminal sentencing. Mandatory minimum prison sentences, sentencing guidelines, parole abolition, and life sentences for third-time felons were widely adopted through the 1980s. The no-nonsense, tough-on-crime politics reached a bipartisan apotheosis with President [Bill] Clinton's 1994 crime bill, which launched the largest prison construction project in the nation's history. As a result of these changes, prison time—as opposed to community supervision—became the main criminal sanction for felony offenders.

Three Fallacies

The failure of the great experiment in mass incarceration is rooted in three fallacies of the tough-on-crime perspective. First, there is the fallacy of us and them. For tough-on-crime advocates, the innocent majority is victimized by a class of predatory criminals, and the prison works to separate us from them. The truth is that the criminals live among us as our young fathers, brothers, and sons. Drug use, fighting, theft, and disorderly conduct are behavioral staples of male youth. Most of the crime they commit is perpetrated on each other. This is reflected most tragically in the high rates of homicide victimization among males under age twenty-five, black males in particular. Some young men do become more seriously and persistently involved in crime, but neither the criminal justice system nor criminologists can predict who those serious offenders will be or when they will stop offending. Thus the power to police and punish cannot separate us from criminals with great distinction, but instead flows along the contours of social inequality. Visible markers like age, skin color, and neighborhood become rough proxies for criminal threat. Small race and class differences in offending are amplified at each stage of criminal processing from arrest through conviction and sentencing. As a result, the prison walls we built with such industry in the 1980s and '90s did not keep out the criminal predators, but instead divided us internally, leaving our poorest communities with fewer opportunities to join the mainstream and deeply skeptical of the institutions charged with their safety.

Second, there is the fallacy of personal defect. Tough-on-crime politics disdains the criminology of root causes and traces crime not to poverty and unemployment but to the moral failures of individuals. Refusing to resist temptation or defer gratification, the offender lacks empathy and affect, lacks human connection, and is thus less human than the rest of us. The diagnosis of defective character points to immutable criminality, stoking cynicism for rehabilitative efforts, and justifying the mission of semipermanent incapacitation. The folk theory of immutable criminality permits the veiled association of crime with race in political talk. But seeking criminality in defects of character, the architects of the prison boom ignored the great rise in urban youth unemployment that preceded the growth in murder rates in the 1960s and '70s. They ignored the illegal drug trade, which flourished to fill the vacuum of legitimate economic opportunity left by urban deindustrialization. They ignored, too, the fact that jobs are not just a source of economic opportunity but of social control that routinizes daily life and draws young men into a wide array of socially beneficial roles. Lastly, they ignored the bonds of mutual assistance that are only weakly sustained by communities of concentrated poverty. Thus young men would return home from prison only to easily surmount once again the same stunted social barriers to crime that contributed to their imprisonment in the first place.

The final fallacy of the tough-on-crime perspective is the myth of the free market. The free market fallacy sees the welfare state as pampering the criminal class and building expectations of something for nothing. Antipoverty programs were trimmed throughout the 1970s and '80s, and poor young men largely fell through the diminished safety net that remained. For free marketeers, the question was simply whether or not to spend public money on the poor—they did not anticipate that idle young men present a social problem. Without school, work, or military service, these poor young men were left on the street corner, sometimes acting disorderly and often fuelling fears of crime. We may have skimped on welfare, but we paid anyway, splurging on police and prisons. Because incarceration was so highly concentrated in particular neighborhoods and areas within them, certain city blocks received millions of dollars in "correctional investment"—spending on the removal of local residents by incarceration. These million-dollar blocks reveal a question falsely posed. We never faced a choice of whether to spend money on the poor; the dollars diverted from education and employment found their way to prison construction. Our political choice, it turned out, was not how much we spent on the poor, but what to spend it on.

| *"Restorative justice acknowledges that crime is about more than breaking the law; therefore, the resolution is about more than simple punishment."*

Restorative Justice Is a Good Alternative to Incarceration

Patrice Gaines

In the following viewpoint, Patrice Gaines argues that for many convicted criminals, there is a promising alternative to incarceration. Drawing on her own experience as a convicted felon, Gaines contends that restorative justice allows offenders a resolution to their crime that avoids the damage done by incarceration. She claims that restorative justice has a long history and that programs around the country are yielding promising results. Gaines is a writer, teacher, speaker, and justice reform activist. She is the author of Laughing in the Dark: From Colored Girl to Woman of Color—A Journey from Prison to Power.

As you read, consider the following questions:

1. The author claims what fraction of the prison population is locked up for nonviolent drug offenses?

2. Gaines gives an example of restorative justice where a youth who stole a car avoids juvenile detention by doing what instead?

3. The author contends that since she started speaking in prisons sixteen years ago, what fact about the detained women has not changed?

It was the summer of 2009. I was on my second day of work for the U.S. Census Bureau, knocking on doors in rural South Carolina.

My cell phone rang. It was my supervisor.

"Patrice, headquarters called me and told me to send you home immediately and to take back all government property," she said. "I don't know why."

She knew me as a 61-year-old gray-haired mother, a former *Washington Post* reporter, an author and motivational speaker. She knew nothing about me 40 years ago, when I was a 21-year-old heroin user. I knew exactly why they were sending me home: I am a convicted felon.

In 1970, I spent part of a summer in jail for a drug charge and received five years of probation. But that was just the beginning. In the decades since, I have learned what it's like to try to change your life in a fearful society that believes it's safest to lock up or discard anyone who has ever made a criminal mistake or had a problem with addiction. And I have learned that there's another way—a way that offers the possibility of restoring dignity and hope both to the people who make mistakes and those victimized by crime.

The Burden of a Criminal Record

The U.S. Department of Justice reports that one in 32 adults in the United States is behind bars or on probation or parole. One-quarter of the prison population is locked up for nonviolent drug offenses, according to the Center for Economic and Policy Research.

Each time a person is locked away behind bars, it leaves a void in a family, neighborhood, or community. Most often, the burden of incarceration falls on communities of color. The Drug Policy Alliance (DPA), a leading organization promoting alternatives to incarceration, writes, "The war on drugs has become a war on families, a war on public health, and a war on our constitutional rights."

"We are exiling millions of mothers, fathers, brothers, sisters, sons, and daughters—making them missing persons," says Carol Fennelly, director of Hope House, a Washington, D.C.-based nonprofit organization that helps children stay connected with incarcerated parents.

I was lucky. I was becoming an addict when I was convicted. The system that sent me to jail did nothing to address my drug problem: It put me on probation and ordered me to pay more than $2,000 in fines, which only made me more bitter. I was a single mother who could not find a job because of my criminal record. I did not see any connection between the high fines and my behavior. I did not see how I was expected to dig myself out of the hole I was in.

Anyone labeled an "offender" or "ex-con" has a difficult time finding employment. Even though I served a short sentence, once I got out of jail, I could not find a job. I didn't know how to answer the question, "Have you ever been convicted of a felony?" Some days I lied; some days I told the truth.

If I lied, I usually got fired within two weeks when the results of the background check came in. If I told the truth, I didn't get past the interview.

I searched for a job for at least three months before I finally received a break: A woman at a mental health center took a chance and hired me to work as a clerk in the business office in spite of my criminal record. Over the next several years, I took creative writing courses at night, got accepted into a journalism training program, and eventually became a newspaper reporter.

But I have never forgotten that those doors probably would never have opened without the woman who was brave enough to give me a chance.

An Alternative to Incarceration

Years later, as a reporter at the *Washington Post,* I wrote my autobiography, *Laughing in the Dark,* and started giving motivational speeches and running workshops for women in prisons around the country.

The more time I spent in prisons, the more I came to believe that there had to be a way to keep our streets safe without throwing people away. Everywhere I turned, I saw myself. I met women, most of them mothers, serving too much time for crimes (embezzlement, check fraud, prostitution, burglary) committed because, like me, they had a drug problem.

Then I discovered what I had been looking for—an alternative to incarceration called restorative justice.

In restorative justice, all of the parties impacted by an offense—offender, victim, and community—are involved in determining a resolution that addresses the harm caused by the crime. Restorative justice acknowledges that crime is about more than breaking the law; therefore, the resolution is about more than simple punishment.

In North America, restorative justice has roots in the very communities that have been hurt most by the prison system. There is evidence that similar approaches were used by West African slaves brought to the Sea Islands of South Carolina and Georgia and by Native Americans.

While researching restorative justice, I found cases such as one in Norfolk, Va., where a youth stole his parents' car, crashed it into another woman's car, and ran. Instead of serving time in juvenile detention, a restorative justice program allowed him to work and pay the woman back for damage to her car and income she lost while her injuries prevented her from working. The youth and the victim met, and he was able

The Restorative Process

Restorative processes offer an alternative, one that con-
nects people by allowing them to not just understand
each other but experience each other's humanity. That's
why restorative acts are offered. That's why they are experienced as restorative. There is nothing like it in our
current ways of doing justice.

Mikhail Lyubansky,
"Our Justice System Requires Us to Punish Wrongdoers.
What If There Were a Better Way?," Psychology Today,
August 18, 2010.

to see the connection between his bad decisions and the harm
he had caused. It struck me that he received what I missed.
He was given work to help him pay his restitution. The process was respectful to everyone: The young man left changed
but not labeled a criminal.

Resolving Crime in the Community

I met Morris Jenkins, a criminal justice scholar at the University of Toledo. Jenkins's work demonstrates how communities
have historically resolved crime. The Sea Islands have preserved much of the unique Gullah culture of the West Afri-
cans who were brought there as slaves generations ago. Jenkins
found that before there was a bridge from the islands to the
mainland, the island people used restorative justice to settle
civil disputes and some criminal complaints. "They called it
the Just Law," Jenkins told me recently. "One of the ladies in
her 90s told me a story about how they used to have these
community meetings at faith houses—little shacks, not
churches. They would bring together the offender and his

folks, and victims and their folks, and the elders—and they would come up with a resolution."

As I investigated these stories, I realized restorative justice offered everything my experience with the corrections system did not. I had wanted to change my life, so I could be a good daughter, sister, and mother. But I didn't know how to change. Being on probation, paying restitution, and being disregarded when I applied for a job did not address my desire to be a good person or help boost my self-esteem. The punishment and judgment against me crippled me even more.

Once I committed my crime, I never felt as if I was part of a community. No one saw the power in getting me to realize the harm I had caused to my family. My parents were ashamed. I disappointed friends and neighbors who had helped me over the years. I knew that some of them probably even felt I had brought shame to our close-knit neighborhood. No one ever considered finding a way for me to give back, to feel forgiven and accepted again. I had to put all of the pieces together myself—find a way to repair the harm I caused, forgive myself, and be a part of the community again—a process that took years.

Restorative Justice Programs

Over the years since I discovered restorative justice, the number of programs has grown slowly. Today, as federal and local governments search for ways to save money, more attention is being paid to alternatives to incarceration. Many restorative justice programs are now operating in partnership with the court system.

My friends, Ivy and Saleem Hylton, receive clients referred by the Court Services and Offender Supervision Agency in Washington, D.C. The couple cofounded Youth and Families in Crisis, which runs innovative restorative justice sessions in Prince George's County, Md.

The Hyltons have seen incredible changes in former perpetrators of violent crimes who have attended their restorative justice sessions. They teach relaxation and meditation to clients to give them tools for controlling their emotions and refocusing their attention. Using a restorative justice practice from Native American traditions, they hold discussion circles in which each person has an opportunity to speak without interruption and learns to truly hear and respect others, often for the first time.

I spoke with Antonio Addison, who spent 15 years in prison for a murder conviction: He believes participating in the circles and learning to meditate has saved his life.

"We started with prayer and then the circle," said Addison. "Some spoke up; some were not open. I would share my deepest emotions. The only peace I had felt in my life was when I was in the hole in prison, in solitary."

Addison found he could create a feeling of peace by using sounds introduced to him at the sessions, such as the sound of the ocean or soft bells. "I would play the CDs to relieve stress before I went to sleep. Then I started using them when I got upset or angry, and I found they relieved me of those things so [my emotions] didn't build up and explode."

In one year, with the Hyltons' help, Addison accomplished something he could not do in 15 years of incarceration: He is able to control his anger before it explodes into rage. Now, at 41, Addison is married, has two-year-old twins, is a supervisor for a major utility company, and gives back by volunteering with the Hyltons, encouraging new participants by sharing his story and answering their questions.

Restoring Hope and Imagination

Five years ago, I cofounded a nonprofit organization, the Brown Angel Center, which helps women transition from prison to the community. We run workshops for the women in the Mecklenburg County Jail in Charlotte, N.C. A couple of months ago, I was teaching the women about restorative justice. They sat silent, intrigued.

"We need that here," one said.

"It makes so much sense," said another.

At the jail, the women are waiting to be sentenced or to begin long prison terms. They are separated from their children, and some have already lost custody because their sentences are too long to allow them to continue parenting. One thing hasn't changed since I started speaking in prisons 16 years ago: Most women I meet are incarcerated for nonviolent crimes. Restorative justice would help them; prison time does not.

Meanwhile, restorative justice practitioners say we have just begun to use our creativity to develop inventive programs to address crime. I speak at colleges around the country, encouraging a new generation of leaders to consider applying their talents to create a new model of justice. I stand before these students and the women who are locked up as an example of the distance one person can travel in a lifetime.

Dressed in my best business suit, I hold up my mug shot to illustrate to them that you can never know what a person might become, what potential they have within. My photo shows me at 21, a baby-faced girl with a large afro and a sign hanging around her neck that says, "Charlotte Mecklenburg NC, 19 Jun 70, 70–90."

"This is what a drug addict looks like," I say. "This is what a teacher looks like. This is what an author looks like. This is what a mother looks like."

"When adequately funded, both probation and parole can be effective for limiting the overall incarcerated population and reducing recidivism."

Probation and Parole
Are Good Alternatives
to Incarceration

America

In the following viewpoint, the editors of America *argue that the
recession of the early twenty-first century provides a good opportunity to consider alternatives to incarceration. They contend
that it would be wise to spend more money on probation and
parole as states consider cutting funding to prisons. In states
where there is prison growth, the editors caution that greater incarceration is not a good long-term strategy for improving public
safety.* America *is a weekly Catholic Jesuit magazine; its editorial
board is made up of both Jesuit priests and brothers, as well as
laypeople.*

As you read, consider the following questions:

1. According to a study cited by the authors, by what percentage has corrections spending increased since 1986?

2. What percentage of correction funds is devoted to incarceration, according to the editors of *America*?

3. The authors claim that the supply of drug dealers will be unlimited unless society does what?

Recession-driven prison closings may provide state lawmakers an opportunity to promote a more rational approach to criminal justice that still puts public safety first. Draconian sentences even for low-level offenders have long crowded penal facilities, and over the past two decades the building of new prisons has increased dramatically. In the 1960s and 70s an average of four prisons a year were under construction, but in the 1990s the average jumped to 24 a year. Correctional costs now swallow up huge portions of many state budgets. According to a March 2009 report by the Pew Center on the States, total corrections spending has reached an estimated $68 billion, an increase of 336 percent since 1986.

The Need for Community Corrections

For some states, this spending has produced disquieting signs of skewed spending priorities. In Michigan, for example, one of the states hit hardest by the recession because of its ties with the ailing automotive industry, the state government spends more on corrections than on higher education, despite having already closed half a dozen penal facilities.

Other states are considering early release for low-level offenders who seem to present little risk to public safety. Arizona, New Jersey and Vermont reduced the sentences of thousands of probation and parole violators who had been returned to prison for violations of various kinds. Early release, though, can work well only if strong reentry programs are in place—initiatives that provide help with housing, jobs and substance abuse. According to Marc Mauer, executive director of the nonprofit Sentencing Project in Washington,

D.C., the commitment to reentry programs has grown over the past decade—a positive sign of a practice he hopes will continue.

Two of the most effective forms of community corrections, probation (after conviction but before incarceration) and parole (for those who have served time and are eligible for release), have long been underfunded. Yet when adequately funded, both probation and parole can be effective for limiting the overall incarcerated population and reducing recidivism. But with nearly 90 percent of corrections funds devoted to incarceration, Mauer points out, only 10 percent remains for probation and parole. In many jurisdictions, caseloads are too high to permit adequate supervision and services for those released. Cuts in those areas are being made by cash-strapped administrators—a case of being penny-wise and pound-foolish. The Pew report notes that in Sacramento County, Calif., 76 probation officer positions, or 9 percent of the total force, are on the chopping block, as are drug treatment beds.

An Increase in Prisons

Not all parts of the country are closing prisons. Parts of the South have been moving in the opposite direction. Florida shows no signs of closing any of its penal facilities. And Kentucky has the fastest growing prison system in the nation because of various tough-on-crime measures, like the so-called persistent felon law, similar to the "three strikes and you're out" laws of some states, as well as such other measures as reclassifying some misdemeanors as felonies, which carry much harsher penalties. Kentucky's prisons have become so overcrowded that it has been obliged to pay local jails to house the overflow, and many inmates sleep on the floor. As the Pew report observes, over-incarceration is subject to the law of diminishing returns; the greater the number of offenders imprisoned, "the lower the payoff in terms of crime reduction." Similarly, incarcerating more offenders can lead to "the replacement effect," especially in regard to drug crimes: Other drug dealers quickly take over the territory left open by the person behind bars. This is especially true of young people, who are more easily drawn into criminal activity than those in their 30s and 40s. So unless society addresses the demand for drugs, the supply of potential sellers seems virtually unlimited.

Corrections officer unions and local communities whose economies depend on prisons have resisted prison closings. In some rural areas, prisons serve as large local employers, and local employment in turn supports a number of small businesses—a chain of economic dependency. Such resistance is understandable, given the paucity of employment opportunities in such regions, but it raises an important question: How many prisons exist because of the secure jobs they provide rather than for the punishment of crime and promotion of public safety? Robert Gangi, who heads the Correctional Association of New York, has noted that the "administration of justice shouldn't be twisted into a job program for economically depressed upstate communities."

It is time to put in place programs and policies that will depend less on funding and political issues, like those that created excessively stringent drug laws, and ensure a more rational, effective approach to public safety.

| *"Just the money costs of turning crimi-
nals loose is enough to show what reckless nonsense is being preached."*

There Are High Costs to Incarceration Alternatives

Thomas Sowell

*In the following viewpoint, Thomas Sowell contends that propos-
als to develop alternatives to incarceration are flawed. Sowell
claims that any money that is saved by avoiding incarceration
ends up being outweighed by the amount of money it costs society to deal with a criminal on the loose. Furthermore, Sowell
contends that opponents of incarceration exaggerate the severity
of punishment criminals receive, claiming that the actual sentences served are usually much less than the sentence given. Sowell is an economist who is the Rose and Milton Friedman Senior
Fellow at the Hoover Institution of Stanford University.*

As you read, consider the following questions:

1. Sowell claims that proponents of the alternative of intensive probation say that five years would cost how
much less than imprisonment?

2. According to the author, in the United States it costs how much less to incarcerate a criminal than to use alternatives?

3. Sowell claims that what four reasons allow criminals to be released before serving the entire length of their original sentence?

For more than 200 years, the political Left has been coming up with reasons why criminals should not be punished as much, or at all. The latest gambit in Missouri is providing judges with the costs of incarcerating the criminals they sentence.

The Push for Alternatives to Incarceration

According to the *New York Times*, "a three-year prison sentence would run more than $37,000 while probation would cost $6,770." For a more serious crime, where a 5-year imprisonment would cost more than $50,000, it would cost less than $9,000 for what is described as "five years of intensive probation."

This is only the latest in a long line of "alternatives to incarceration" schemes that are constantly being pushed by all sorts of clever people, not only in Missouri but across the United States and across the Atlantic, especially in Britain.

The most obvious question that is being resolutely ignored in these scientific-sounding calculations is: What is the cost of turning criminals loose? Phrases like "intensive probation" may create the illusion that criminals at large are somehow under control of the authorities but illusions are especially dangerous when it comes to crime.

The Cost of Turning Criminals Loose

Another question that ought to be obvious is: Why are we counting only the cost to the government of putting a criminal behind bars, but not the cost to the public of turning him loose?

Some may say that it is not possible to quantify the costs of the dangers and anxieties of the public when more criminals are walking the streets. That is certainly true, if you mean the full costs. But we can quantify the money costs—and just the money costs to the public vastly exceed the costs to the government of locking up criminals.

In Britain, where the "alternatives to incarceration" vogue has led to only 7 percent of convicted criminals being put behind bars, the annual cost of the prison system has been estimated at just under two billion pounds sterling. Meanwhile, the annual financial cost alone of crimes committed against the public has been an estimated sixty billion pounds sterling.

In the United States, the cost of incarcerating a criminal has been estimated as being $10,000 a year less than the cost of turning him loose.

In all these calculations we are leaving out the costs of violence, intimidation and the fears that people have for the safety of themselves and their children, not to mention the sense of helplessness and outrage when society refuses to pay as much attention to innocent victims as they lavish on the criminals who victimize them.

These are all important costs. But it is unnecessary to take them into account, when just the money costs of turning criminals loose is enough to show what reckless nonsense is being preached to us by arrogant elites in the media, in academia and elsewhere.

The Reality of Sentences

Deception of the public by advocates of leniency to criminals has been institutionalized in legal practices that create the illusion of far more punishment being meted out than is actually the case. "Concurrent sentences" are one of the most blatant of these frauds.

When a criminal has been convicted of multiple crimes, having him serve his sentences for these crimes "concurrently" means that he actually serves no more time for five crimes than he would serve for whichever of those crimes has the longest sentence. In other words, the other four crimes are "on the house."

Sentences in general overstate how long the criminal will actually spend behind bars. Probation, furloughs, parole and time off for good behavior lead the list of reasons for turning a criminal loose before he serves the sentence that was announced to the public when he was convicted.

Even "life imprisonment without the possibility of parole"—often offered as a substitute for execution for first degree murder—can be misleading. There is no such thing as life imprisonment without the possibility of a liberal governor being elected, and then commuting or pardoning the murderer later on. And, of course, the murderer can commit murder again behind bars.

With all the things that liberals are willing to spend vast sums of money on, it is a little much to have them become penny-wise when it comes to keeping criminals off the streets.

Periodical and Internet Sources Bibliography

The following articles have been selected to supplement the diverse views presented in this chapter.

Michelle Alexander	"The New Jim Crow," *Huffington Post*, February 8, 2010. www.huffingtonpost.com.
Radley Balko	"The Crime Rate Puzzle," *Reason*, July 2011.
Atul Gawande	"Hellhole," *New Yorker*, March 30, 2009.
Scott Horton	"'In Defense of Flogging': Six Questions for Peter Moskos," *Harper's*, July 2011.
Peter Katel	"Downsizing Prisons," *CQ Researcher*, March 11, 2011.
Glenn Loury	"A Nation of Jailers," *Cato Unbound*, March 11, 2009. www.cato-unbound.org.
Mikhail Lyubansky	"Our Justice System Requires Us to Punish Wrongdoers. What If There Were a Better Way?," *Psychology Today*, August 18, 2010.
Marc Mauer	"Addressing Racial Disparities in Incarceration," *Prison Journal*, September 12, 2011.
Neal Peirce	"America Behind Bars: The Time Is Ripe for Prison Reform," *Seattle Times*, August 15, 2010.
Amanda Petteruti and Nastassia Walsh	"Jailing Communities: The Impact of Jail Expansion and Effective Public Safety Strategies," Justice Policy Institute, April 2008. www.justicepolicy.org.
Liliana Segura	"Michelle Alexander on California's 'Cruel and Unusual' Prisons," *Nation*, May 26, 2011.
Bruce Western	"Locked Up, Locked Out: The Social Costs of Incarceration," *Reason*, July 2011.

CHAPTER 3

Should Sentencing Laws Be Reformed?

Chapter Preface

When criminals are convicted of crimes, courts must determine the appropriate punishment during the sentencing phase. Punishment can include fines, incarceration, probation, a suspended sentence that would take effect if probation were violated, payment of restitution to the victim, community service, or drug and alcohol rehabilitation. Factors that affect sentencing include the convict's criminal history, the nature of the crime, and other circumstances of the convict, including age. In recent years, the US Supreme Court has grappled with several cases concerning the constitutionality of sentences imposed on minors, most recently ruling on the constitutionality of the sentence of life without parole for juvenile offenders.

In 2010 the US Supreme Court decided in *Graham v. Florida* that juvenile offenders may not be sentenced to life imprisonment without the possibility of parole for non-homicide offenses. The case involved a sixteen-year-old who—charged as an adult—had pled guilty to the charge of armed burglary with assault and battery, a first-degree felony punishable by a life sentence. Justice Anthony Kennedy, writing for the majority, concluded:

> The Constitution prohibits the imposition of a life without parole sentence on a juvenile offender who did not commit homicide. A State need not guarantee the offender eventual release, but if it imposes a sentence of life it must provide him or her with some realistic opportunity to obtain release before the end of that term.

The court here draws a sharp distinction between the kinds of sentences appropriate for adults and those appropriate for juveniles, noting, "The juvenile should not be deprived of the opportunity to achieve maturity of judgment and self-recognition of human worth and potential."

The *Graham v. Florida* decision followed on the heels of the court's 2005 decision in *Roper v. Simmons*, which determined that it is unconstitutional to give minors under the age of eighteen a sentence of death. The court ruled that the death sentence for minors constitutes a violation of the Eighth Amendment's protection against "cruel and unusual punishments." The *Roper* decision upheld the court's earlier reasoning in *Thompson v. Oklahoma* (1988) that capital punishment for a fifteen-year-old minor convicted of murder amounts to cruel and unusual punishment. But a year later in the case of *Stanford v. Kentucky* (1989), the court ruled that death penalty sentences for sixteen- and seventeen-year-olds convicted of murder were not cruel and unusual punishment. The *Roper* decision, then, overruled the 1989 *Stanford* decision.

The impact of the court's decisions on the constitutionality of juvenile sentencing remains to be seen. The court's finding that certain sentences constitute a violation of the Eighth Amendment opens the door for other juvenile sentences to come into question. It also remains to be seen how the court's reasoning could be extended to rulings on the constitutionality of sentencing for adults. In the following chapter, commentators debate the efficacy and constitutionality of the death penalty, life-without-parole sentences, and other severe punishments.

> *"The greatest argument in favor of a moratorium on the death penalty rests in the overwhelming evidence that the system is consistently error bound and flawed."*

The Death Penalty Should Be Abolished

John W. Whitehead

In the following viewpoint, John W. Whitehead argues that the death penalty system in America is flawed to a degree that warrants abolishing capital punishment. Whitehead claims that the evidence of errors in capital cases, the racial disparities in sentencing, the trial and execution costs of death penalty cases, the lack of evidence of a deterrent effect, and the large number of innocent people already killed support elimination of this criminal justice practice. Whitehead is an attorney, author, and founder of the Rutherford Institute, a nonprofit civil liberties and human rights organization.

As you read, consider the following questions:

1. According to Whitehead, what are the four countries that execute more people than the United States?

2. Black defendants are how much more likely than white defendants to be sentenced to death, according to the author?

3. Whitehead claims that since 1973, how many people have been released from death row after their innocence was brought to light?

There is nothing moral or just about the death penalty—certainly not the way it is implemented in America, and anyone who says otherwise is either deluding themselves or trying to get elected by appearing tough on crime. Take Troy Davis, for example, a 43-year-old black man from Georgia who has spent the past 20 years of his life on death row for allegedly shooting and killing a white off-duty police officer—a crime he very well may not have committed.

A Troubling Death Penalty Case

According to Amnesty International, the case against Davis consisted entirely of witness testimony, which contained inconsistencies even at the time of the trial. Since then, all but two of the state's non-police witnesses from the trial have recanted or contradicted their testimony. Many of these witnesses have stated in sworn affidavits that they were pressured or coerced by police into testifying or signing statements against Troy Davis. One of the two witnesses who has not recanted his testimony is Sylvester "Red" Coles—the principal alternative suspect, according to the defense, against whom there is new evidence implicating him as the gunman. Nine individuals have signed affidavits implicating Sylvester Coles.

Despite the fact that the case against Davis has largely fallen apart, the courts have not been inclined to grant Davis a new trial or evidentiary hearing. At a minimum, there's enough doubt as to Davis' guilt to commute his sentence. And even with prominent politicians and public officials such as former president Jimmy Carter, Pope Benedict XVI and [retired South African archbishop] Desmond Tutu lobbying on his behalf, Davis continues to languish on death row at a Georgia prison.

Unfortunately, Davis' journey to death row and his impending execution are indicative of the many failings of the capital punishment system in America, a system sorely lacking in justice and riddled by racial prejudice and economic inequality, not to mention outright corruption. [Editor's note: Davis was executed on September 21, 2011.]

Countries and States with the Death Penalty

As it now stands, America's Western allies have abolished the death penalty, leaving America as one of only three industrialized democracies still carrying out capital punishment. Internationally, the U.S. ranks fifth in terms of the number of prisoners put to death, putting America in such ill-esteemed company as the regimes of China, Iran, North Korea, and Yemen. In fact, Mahmoud Ahmadinejad, the president of Iran, wasted no time in pointing out the hypocrisy of the U.S. executing Teresa Lewis [a woman convicted of arranging the murders of her husband and stepson] last year [2010] while criticizing Iran for stoning a woman convicted of adultery.

Within the U.S., 14 states and the District of Columbia have done away with the death penalty. Execution remains an option in 34 states and for federal inmates. Of the states still actively putting prisoners to death, Texas and Virginia rank highest for the number of executions carried out since capital punishment was reinstated in 1976. Indeed, Texas governor Rick Perry has presided over more than 200 executions during his time in office, more than any other governor in U.S. history, while Virginia governor Bob McDonnell has been an outspoken, staunch supporter of the death penalty. Contrast this with Illinois governor Pat Quinn who, on March 9, 2011, signed a law banning the death penalty, saying it was impos-

The Issue of Deterrence

The death penalty has no deterrent effect. Former claims that each execution deters a certain number of murders have been thoroughly discredited by social science research. People commit murders largely in the heat of passion, under the influence of alcohol or drugs, or because they are mentally ill, giving little or no thought to the possible consequences of their acts. The few murderers who plan their crimes beforehand—for example, professional executioners—intend and expect to avoid punishment altogether by not getting caught.

American Civil Liberties Union (ACLU), "The Death Penalty: Questions and Answers," September 2011. www.aclu.org.

sible to fix a system that had wrongly condemned at least 20 innocent men to death (138 death row inmates have had their convictions overturned since the death penalty was reinstated in 1976). New York, New Jersey and New Mexico have also done away with capital punishment in the past two years.

Evidence of a Flawed System

Thus far, the greatest argument in favor of a moratorium on the death penalty rests in the overwhelming evidence that the system is consistently error bound and flawed. In a Columbia University study on 5,760 capital cases, the report found an overall rate of error of 68 percent. In other words, courts found serious reversible errors in nearly 7 out of 10 capital cases. The most common errors included egregiously incompetent defense lawyers, prosecutorial suppression of evidence and other misconduct, misinstruction of juries, and biased judges and juries. As U.S. Supreme Court justice Ruth Bader Ginsburg once observed, "I have yet to see a death case among the dozens coming to the Supreme Court on eve-of-execution stay applications in which the defendant was well represented at trial. . . . People who are well represented at trial do not get the death penalty."

In the Columbia University study, the team of legal analysts concluded that the death penalty system was "collapsing under the weight of its own mistakes. They reveal a system in which lives and public order are at stake, yet for decades has made more mistakes than we would tolerate in far less important activities. They reveal a system that is wasteful and broken and needs to be addressed."

Disparities in Sentencing

The racial disparities in sentencing are well known. For example, there are 1,371 blacks on death row (42% of the total death row population) despite the fact that blacks only make up 12% of the U.S. population. Indeed, blacks are 40% more likely to be sentenced to death than a white defendant who has committed the same crime. Class and wealth are also a factor in who receives the death penalty. In fact, almost all death row inmates could not afford their own attorney at trial and there is a significant disparity in wealth between murderers who live and those who are executed.

Those who end up on death row are also often the products of extreme abuse or abject poverty. "In the US the overwhelming majority of those executed are psychotic, alcoholic, drug addicted or mentally unstable," said George Ryan, former Illinois governor. "They frequently are raised in an impoverished and abusive environment. Seldom are people with money or prestige convicted of capital offenses, even more seldom are they executed."

The Practical Considerations

Rejection of the death penalty arises from many practical considerations as well. Abolishing the death penalty would save money to fund public works programs to reduce poverty and child abuse, or simply to reduce taxes and put more money in the pockets of Americans. The death penalty, however, costs the state a great deal of money. Some studies estimate that states spend 48% to 300% more prosecuting cases in which the death penalty is an option versus cases in which it is not. In North Carolina, it costs more than $2 million to execute just *one* person. There are a myriad of ways to better utilize the money presently being spent on prosecuting, sentencing, and appealing death penalty cases.

As for the argument that the death penalty is a deterrent to future violent crimes, there is no convincing evidence to support that claim. Indeed, 67% of U.S. police chiefs do not believe that the death penalty significantly reduces the numbers of murders. One study determined that there was no appreciable difference in murder rates before and after states had either reinstated or abolished the death penalty. Due to the slow process and infrequent occurrence of death sentences being carried out throughout the United States, most regression analysis studies are unable to prove the efficacy of the death sentence. As Gregory Ruff, a police lieutenant in Kansas, noted, "I have never heard a murderer say they thought about the death penalty as consequence of their actions prior to committing their crimes."

The Killing of Innocent People

Furthermore, the death penalty allows government officials, who are often corrupt or misinformed, to pursue an irreversible policy of killing with imperfect information. Consequently, police officers, prosecutors, juries, and judges have sent many innocent men to death row. Since 1973, 138 people have been released from death row after evidence of their innocence was brought to light, each person spending an average of 9.8 years in prison. That amounts to one in every ten prisoners condemned to die since 1976 being innocent. Yet human nature and the law of averages decree that if more than 100 individuals have prevailed in proving their innocence, there must be many more who have not been able to do so. Whether through lack of resources, opportunity or time, these individuals go to their deaths innocent of the crimes for which they were charged.

One such person is Cameron Todd Willingham, accused, tried, and convicted of setting a fire that killed his three children in 1992. He was put on death row and executed in 2004. However, since his death there has been a rigorous investigation into the circumstances surrounding the fire that suggests Willingham was, in fact, innocent.

Even if most of those condemned to die prove to be guilty, if just one innocent person is wrongly executed, that is still one too many. No matter what our individual views on the death penalty, its application clearly deserves closer scrutiny. "Our capital system is haunted by the demon of error," Governor George Ryan once said, "error in determining guilt and error in determining who among the guilty deserves to die." The inconsistency and utter randomness of imposing the death penalty by any governmental body should give even the most hard-line death penalty advocate pause.

| "The criminal process should not be abused to prevent the lawful imposition of the death penalty in appropriate capital cases."

The Death Penalty Should Not Be Abolished

David Muhlhausen

In the following viewpoint, David Muhlhausen argues that there is a sound justification for having the death penalty as an option within the criminal justice system. Muhlhausen claims that despite objections to the contrary, the death penalty in America is not racially discriminatory. He argues that both past and current research supports the view that allowing capital punishment saves lives by deterring would-be criminals. Thus, he concludes that Americans are justified in supporting the death penalty. Muhlhausen is a research fellow at the Heritage Foundation's Center for Data Analysis.

As you read, consider the following questions:

1. According to the author, Americans support the death penalty by what ratio?

David Muhlhausen, "The Death Penalty Deters Crime and Saves Lives," Hearing Before the Subcommittee on the Constitution, Civil Rights and Human Rights of the Committee on the Judiciary, US Senate, 110th Congress, 1st Session, June 27, 2007, pp. 271–277.

2. Muhlhausen cites research done on data from 1977 to 1996 showing that each execution, on average, results in how many fewer murders?

3. The author claims that each additional execution in the United States deters the murder of how many African Americans?

While opponents of capital punishment have been very vocal in their opposition, Gallup opinion polls consistently demonstrate that the American public overwhelmingly supports capital punishment. In Gallup's most recent [2006] poll, 67 percent of Americans favor the death penalty for those convicted of murder, while only 28 percent are opposed. From 2000 to the most recent poll in 2006, support for capital punishment consistently runs a 2:1 ratio in favor.

Despite strong public support for capital punishment, federal, state, and local officials must continually ensure that its implementation rigorously upholds constitutional protections, such as due process and equal protection of the law. However, the criminal process should not be abused to prevent the lawful imposition of the death penalty in appropriate capital cases.

Alleged Racial Discrimination in Capital Punishment Sentences

As of December 2005, there were 37 prisoners under a sentence of death in the federal system. Of these prisoners, 43.2 percent were white, while 54.1 percent were African American. The fact that African Americans are a majority of federal prisoners on death row and a minority in the overall United States population may lead some to conclude that the federal system discriminates against African Americans. However, there is little rigorous evidence that such disparities exist in the federal system.

Under a competitive grant process, the National Institute of Justice awarded the RAND Corporation a grant to determine whether racial disparities exist in the federal death penalty system. The resulting 2006 RAND study set out to determine what factors, including the defendant's race, victim's race, and crime characteristics, affect the decision to seek a death penalty case. Three independent teams of researchers were tasked with developing their own methodologies to analyze the data. Only after each team independently drew their own conclusions did they share their findings with each other.

When first looking at the raw data without controlling for case characteristics, RAND found that large race effects with the decision to seek the death penalty are more likely to occur when the defendants are white and when the victims are white. However, these disparities disappeared in each of the three studies when the heinousness of the crimes was taken into account. The RAND study concludes that the findings support the view that decisions to seek the death penalty are driven by characteristics of crimes rather than by race. RAND's findings are very compelling because three independent research teams, using the same data but different methodologies, reached the same conclusions.

Evidence of Discrimination

While there is little evidence that the federal capital punishment system treats minorities unfairly, some may argue that the death penalty systems in certain states may be discriminatory. One such state is Maryland. In May 2001, the then governor Parris Glendening instituted a moratorium on the use of capital punishment in Maryland in light of concerns that it may be unevenly applied to minorities, especially African Americans. In 2000, Governor Glendening commissioned University of Maryland professor of criminology Ray Paternoster to study the possibility of racial discrimination in the application of the death penalty in Maryland. The results of Professor Paternoster's study found that black defendants who murder white victims are substantially more likely to be charged with a capital crime and sentenced to death.

In 2003, Governor Robert L. Ehrlich wisely lifted the moratorium. His decision was justified. In 2005, a careful review of the study by professor of statistics and sociology Richard Berk of the University of California, Los Angeles and his coauthors found that the results of Professor Paternoster's study do not stand up to statistical scrutiny. According to Professor Berk's reanalysis, "For both capital charges and death sentences, race either played no role or a small role that is very difficult to specify. In short, it is very difficult to find convincing evidence for racial effects in the Maryland data and if there are any, they may not be additive." Further, race may have a small influence because "cases with a black defendant and white victim or 'other' racial combination are *less* likely to have a death sentence."

The Deterrent Effect of the Death Penalty

Federal, state, and local officials need to recognize that the death penalty saves lives. How capital punishment affects murder rates can be explained through general deterrence theory, which supposes that increasing the risk of apprehension and punishment for crime deters individuals from committing crime. Nobel laureate Gary S. Becker's seminal 1968 study of the economics of crime assumed that individuals respond to the costs and benefits of committing crime.

According to deterrence theory, criminals are no different from law-abiding people. Criminals "rationally maximize their own self-interest (utility) subject to constraints (prices, incomes) that they face in the marketplace and elsewhere." Individuals make their decisions based on the net costs and benefits of each alternative. Thus, deterrence theory provides a basis for analyzing how capital punishment should influence murder rates. Over the years, several studies have demonstrated a link between executions and decreases in murder rates. In fact, studies done in recent years, using sophisticated panel data methods, consistently demonstrate a strong link between executions and reduced murder incidents.

Early Research. The rigorous examination of the deterrent effect of capital punishment began with research in the 1970s by Isaac Ehrlich, currently a University of Buffalo Distinguished Professor of Economics. Professor Ehrlich's research found that the death penalty had a strong deterrent effect. While his research was debated by other scholars, additional research by Professor Ehrlich reconfirmed his original findings. In addition, research by Professor Stephen K. Layson of the University of North Carolina at Greensboro strongly reconfirmed Ehrlich's previous findings.

Recent Research. Numerous studies published over the past few years, using panel data sets and sophisticated social science techniques, are demonstrating that the death penalty saves lives. Panel studies observe multiple units over several periods. The addition of multiple data collection points gives the results of capital punishment panel studies substantially more credibility than the results of studies that have only single before-and-after intervention measures. Further, the longitudinal nature of the panel data allows researchers to analyze the impact of the death penalty over time that cross-sectional data sets cannot address.

Recent Data on Deterrence

Using a panel data set of over 3,000 counties from 1977 to 1996, Professors Hashem Dezhbakhsh, Paul H. Rubin, and Joanna M. Shepherd of Emory University found that each execution, on average, results in 18 fewer murders. Using state-level panel data from 1960 to 2000, Professors Dezhbakhsh and Shepherd were able to compare the relationship between executions and murder incidents before, during, and after the U.S. Supreme Court's death penalty moratorium. They found

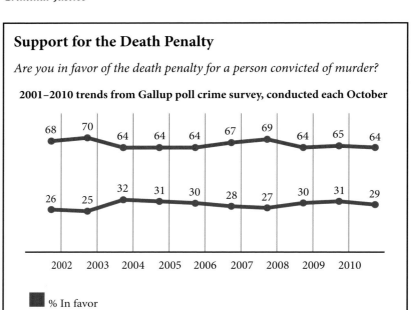

Support for the Death Penalty

Are you in favor of the death penalty for a person convicted of murder?

2001–2010 trends from Gallup poll crime survey, conducted each October

68 70 64 64 64 67 69 64 65 64

26 25 32 31 30 28 27 30 31 29

2002 2003 2004 2005 2006 2007 2008 2009 2010

■ % In favor
■ % Opposed

TAKEN FROM: Frank Newport, "In U.S., 64% Support Death Penalty in Cases of Murder," Gallup, November 8, 2010.

that executions had a highly significant negative relationship with murder incidents. Additionally, the implementation of state moratoria is associated with the increased incidence of murders.

Separately, Professor Shepherd's analysis of monthly data from 1977 to 1999 found three important findings.

First, each execution, on average, is associated with three fewer murders. The deterred murders included both crimes of passion and murders by intimates.

Second, executions deter the murder of whites and African Americans. Each execution prevents the murder of one white person, 1.5 African Americans, and 0.5 persons of other races.

Third, shorter waits on death row are associated with increased deterrence. For each additional 2.75-year reduction in the death row wait until execution, one murder is deterred.

Professors H. Naci Mocan and R. Kaj Gittings of the University of Colorado at Denver have published two studies confirming the deterrent effect of capital punishment. The first study used state-level data from 1977 to 1997 to analyze the influence of executions, commutations, and removals from death row on the incidence of murder. For each additional execution, on average, about five murders were deterred. Alternatively, for each additional commutation, on average, five additional murders resulted. A removal from death row by either state courts or the U.S. Supreme Court is associated with an increase of one additional murder. Addressing criticism of their work, Professors Mocan and Gittings conducted additional analyses and found that their original findings provided robust support for the deterrent effect of capital punishment.

Two studies by Paul R. Zimmerman, a Federal Communications Commission economist, also support the deterrent effect of capital punishment. Using state-level data from 1978 to 1997, Zimmerman found that each additional execution, on average, results in 14 fewer murders. Zimmerman's second study, using similar data, found that executions conducted by electrocution are the most effective at providing deterrence.

Using a small state-level data set from 1995 to 1999, Professor Robert B. Ekelund of Auburn University and his colleagues analyzed the effect that executions have on single incidents of murder and multiple incidents of murder. They found that executions reduced single murder rates, while there was no effect on multiple murder rates.

A Moral Justification

In summary, the recent studies using panel data techniques have confirmed what we learned decades ago: Capital punishment does, in fact, save lives. Each additional execution appears to deter between three and 18 murders. While opponents of capital punishment allege that it is unfairly used against African Americans, each additional execution deters the murder of 1.5 African Americans. Further moratoria, commuted sentences, and death row removals appear to increase the incidence of murder.

The strength of these findings has caused some legal scholars, originally opposed to the death penalty on moral grounds, to rethink their case. In particular, Professor Cass R. Sunstein of the University of Chicago has commented:

> If the recent evidence of deterrence is shown to be correct, then opponents of capital punishment will face an uphill struggle on moral grounds. If each execution is saving lives, the harms of capital punishment would have to be very great to justify its abolition, far greater than most critics have heretofore alleged.

Americans support capital punishment for two good reasons. First, there is little evidence to suggest that minorities are treated unfairly. Second, capital punishment produces a strong deterrent effect that saves lives.

> "The text and history of the Eighth
> Amendment . . . provide little support
> for the idea that life without parole for
> juvenile offenders constitutes prohibited
> 'cruel and unusual' punishment."

Life-Without-Parole Sentences Are Constitutional, Even for Juveniles

Charles D. Stimson and Andrew M. Grossman

In the following viewpoint, Charles D. Stimson and Andrew M. Grossman argue that the Eighth Amendment's prohibition on cruel and unusual punishment does not preclude the criminal justice system from sentencing juveniles to life in prison. Referencing recent US Supreme Court cases, Stimson and Grossman contend that life imprisonment is not analogous to the death penalty, which has been found to be an unconstitutional punishment for minors. Stimson is a senior legal fellow and Grossman is a visiting legal fellow at the Heritage Foundation's Center for Legal and Judicial Studies.

Charles D. Stimson and Andrew M. Grossman, "Adult Time for Adult Crimes: Life Without Parole for Juvenile Killers and Violent Teens," Heritage Foundation, August 2009, pp. 23–39. Copyright © 2009 by the Heritage Foundation. All rights reserved. Reproduced by permission.

As you read, consider the following questions:

1. According to the authors, in what case did the US Supreme Court develop its "narrow proportionality principle" for assessing constitutionality under the Eighth Amendment?

2. Stimson and Grossman claim that what percentage of states have and use life-without-parole sentences for juvenile offenders?

3. At least how many countries around the world have life-without-parole sentences for juvenile offenders, according to the authors?

In 2005, the Supreme Court held in *Roper v. Simmons* that the Eighth and Fourteenth Amendments to the U.S. Constitution bar the application of the death penalty to offenders who were under the age of 18 when their crimes were committed. Since then, the decision's reasoning has become the cornerstone of the efforts of those who oppose life without parole for juvenile offenders and has reinvigorated their legal crusade to put an end to the practice.

The text and history of the Eighth Amendment, however, provide little support for the idea that life without parole for juvenile offenders constitutes prohibited "cruel and unusual" punishment. Even departing from the text and employing a *Roper*-style analysis is unavailing; the factors that the court considered in that case all mitigate in favor of life without parole's constitutionality, even as applied to juvenile offenders.

The Eighth Amendment

The meaning of the Eighth Amendment's prohibition on "cruel and unusual punishments," as incorporated against the states through the Fourteenth Amendment, has been the subject of much disagreement in the literature and in the courts. Its text derives from the English Bill of Rights of 1689, which was well known to legislatures in the American colonies, and later those of the states, and to the framers of the Constitution.

Under the English Bill of Rights, the text merely banned punishments that had not been authorized by Parliament or legal precedent. In the colonies, however, it took on a broader meaning, encompassing as well "cruel methods of punishment that are not regularly or customarily employed" [*Harmelin v. Michigan* (1991)] and are "design[ed] to inflict pain for pain's sake," as had previously been prevalent in Britain and were contemporaneously employed in "less enlightened countries" [*Baze v. Rees* (2008) (Thomas, J., concurring)]. The absence of such a prohibition from the Constitution as drafted in 1787 was a point of contention at several ratifying conventions, and the Eighth Amendment's inclusion in the Bill of Rights was a direct response to these concerns.

Understood in this light, the Eighth Amendment's prohibition extends to torturous *methods* of punishment like "pillorying, disemboweling, decapitation, and drawing and quartering" [*Harmelin*]. The Supreme Court's earliest jurisprudence applying the amendment adopted this view. Thus, the court upheld execution by firing squad and by electrocution, ruling that neither embodied the "something inhuman and barbarous" [*In re Kemmler* (1890)] that the amendment forbids. In the death penalty context, "cruel and unusual" was long seen as encompassing "only such modes of execution as compound the simple infliction of death with added cruelties or indignities" [*Baze*].

Applying that basic formulation to life without parole demonstrates the Eighth Amendment's impotence in the instant policy debate. It is wholly inapplicable. Imprisonment of juveniles has a long historical pedigree, well predating this nation's founding and extending to the present time. Yet there is no suggestion that the *duration* of incarceration, as opposed to the *conditions* in which it is carried out, could be "inhuman and barbarous."

Further, life without parole, unlike a "cruel and unusual" punishment, is not designed to inflict torture as a means of enhancing the punishment; it simply lacks "the evil that the Eighth Amendment targets—intentional infliction of gratuitous pain." Without any aspect of "unnecessary cruelty," the Eighth Amendment is simply unavailing.

While the reasoning of courts in the present era may not track this understanding, the effect remains the same: The courts simply refuse to second-guess the punishments that legislatures prescribe, at least not on Eighth Amendment grounds. Only very rarely is that appropriate deference upset.

The Narrow Proportionality Principle

Yet a majority of the Supreme Court has declined to limit its interpretation to the Eighth Amendment's original meaning. In these cases, the court has held that the Eighth Amendment also prohibits punishments that it has declared to be disproportionate or excessive. Though initially this inquiry was grounded, at least rhetorically, on the comparison of punishments for different statutory offenses—for example, that it was cruel and unusual that punishment for a misrepresentation on a form exceed that available for treason, rebellion, and most homicides—greater theoretical complexity quickly emerged.

The Supreme Court's present formulation of the standard takes two forms. One is a "narrow proportionality principle," applicable in noncapital cases, designed to further judicial economy and deference to the political branches, and buttressed by a more searching but still "objective" analysis of comparative proportionality. The other, so far applicable only to capital punishment, was developed in *Atkins* [*v. Virginia* (2002)] and *Roper* and employs three factors, each one a wide-ranging inquiry.

The "narrow" principle is derived from the court's fractured holding in *Harmelin v. Michigan*. The Eighth Amendment, wrote Justice Anthony Kennedy in a concurrence that the lower courts have taken as controlling, "does not require strict proportionality between crime and sentence," but rather "forbids only extreme sentences that are grossly disproportionate to the crime." This threshold inquiry, a simple comparison of the crime (not the criminal) and the punishment, is as far as most courts need go; a more searching proportionality analysis is "appropriate only in the rare case" in which comparison "leads to an inference of gross disproportionality."

In *Harmelin*, the court upheld a sentence of life without parole for the crime of possession of a large amount of cocaine. Because this crime "threatened to cause grave harm to society," the state legislature "could with reason conclude" that it was "momentous enough to warrant the deterrence and retribution of a life sentence without parole"—a conclusion buttressed by the laws of other states and prior guidance by the court on proportionality.

This appropriately deferential inquiry, focused on the relationship between the crime and the punishment and explicitly rejecting the contention that the Eighth Amendment "mandate[s] adoption of any one penological theory" (such as rehabilitation), affords no room for consideration of the offender's age or maturity. Indeed, a majority of the court held that there is no constitutional right, outside of capital cases, for *any* mitigating factors to be considered in sentencing.

Factors in Sentencing

Only in the rare cases where an inference of disproportionality arises should courts look beyond that relationship, considering three "objective factors": again, the "gravity of the offense and the harshness of the penalty"; sentences imposed on other criminals within the same jurisdiction; and "sentences imposed for commission of the same crime in other jurisdictions" [*Solem v. Helm* (1983)]. Once again, this analysis, focused on "the harm caused or threatened to the victim or society" in assessing the proportionality of the sentence, allows no room for consideration of mitigating factors, such as age, except as may be inherent in assessing the offender's *mens rea*, or criminal intent.

The court reaffirmed the *Harmelin* approach in *Ewing v. California* [(2003)], a challenge to California's three-strikes law by a repeat offender imprisoned for 25 years to life after shoplifting three golf clubs. Nothing in the Eight Amendment, the plurality opinion explained, prohibits the California legislature from "mak[ing] a judgment that protecting the public safety requires incapacitating criminals who have already been convicted of at least one serious or violent crime." It was enough that the state "had a reasonable basis for believing that [the law] advances the goals of its criminal justice system in any substantial way"—in other words, that its justification was not a pretext.

Proportionality analysis as it exists today is no barrier to the imposition of life-without-parole sentences on juvenile offenders so long as the sentence is not enacted for pretextual reasons and is not grossly disproportionate to the crime. There is no evidence or even accusation of pretext, and because the sentence is employed sparingly, in response to only the most grievous conduct, no serious claim can be made that its application is so disproportionate as to preclude its use altogether. Under current law, which enforces a strict separation between capital and noncapital Eighth Amendment law, this would be the end of the analysis.

The Consensus on Punishment

Faced with the insusceptibility of noncapital proportionality analysis to direct consideration of an offender's age, opponents of life without parole for juvenile offenders attempt to extend the court's capital jurisprudence, particularly *Roper*, to noncapital cases; but even this more giving standard (which the court, in any case, seems ill disposed to apply outside of capital cases) would be unavailing. The court in *Roper* actually relies on the existence of the sentence of life without parole for juvenile offenders to reach its result.

Roper employs a three-factor test to determine whether a punishment is constitutionally proportional. The first factor is "objective indicia" of "evolving standards of decency," particularly evidence of a national consensus against the challenged punishment. This is primarily a numerical inquiry, though the relevant types of numbers have varied from case to case.

Roper, similar to *Atkins* before it, focused on three sets of numbers: the number of states allowing or prohibiting the practice; the frequency of the practice in each state (to knock out some states that allow it but use it infrequently); and the recent trend among states that had changed their practices. Thus, in *Roper,* though 20 states, including some of the most populous, allowed the juvenile death penalty and 12 of the remaining 30 had banned the death penalty altogether, the court put greater weight on the fact that only three had used it in the previous decade. The court also found significant a "consistency of direction" in states banning the juvenile death penalty; that is, several had abolished it in recent years, and none that previously prohibited it had reversed course. These numbers—and primarily the "consistency of direction"—demonstrated a "national consensus" that "today our society views juveniles . . . as categorically less culpable than the average criminal," at least as regards the death penalty.

The Issues of Retribution and Deterrence

The second factor—and one that is especially resistant to quantitative or logical analysis—is the "exercise of our own independent judgment" with respect to the proportionality of the challenged punishment. In this inquiry, death is different. As the court put it, "the Eighth Amendment applies to it [the death penalty] with special force." Death was to be reserved for the worst of the worst, a group that cannot include juvenile offenders because they lack maturity and responsibility, are more vulnerable or susceptible to negative influences and outside pressures, and, in terms of character, are both more transitory than and "not as well formed" as adults. Thus, a juvenile's "irresponsible conduct is not as morally reprehensible as that of an adult."

From this, the court concludes that subjecting juvenile offenders to the death penalty does not proportionally further the state's penological justifications: retribution and deterrence. Retribution is undermined because juveniles' ultimate moral culpability is diminished, making the exercise of society's greatest punishment a disproportionate response, and deterrence is uncertain "because the same characteristics that render juveniles less culpable than adults suggest as well that juveniles will be less susceptible to deterrence." Further, the marginal deterrent effect would be no more than "residual," given the availability of "life imprisonment without the possibility of parole," which the court described as "itself a severe sanction, in particular for a young person."

It is worth emphasizing, then, that the *Roper* court relies on the practice of life without parole for juvenile offenders to conclude that the death penalty may be a poor deterrent and so is disproportionate.

Third, the court puts great weight on international law and the practices of foreign countries, an approach sometimes called "transnationalism." These sources are "instructive for its interpretation" of the Eighth Amendment, though not "controlling." In *Roper*, the court specifically considered "the overwhelming weight of international opinion against the juvenile death penalty," as well as the trend among foreign countries. Seemingly most persuasive to the court was the fact "that the United States now stands alone in a world that has turned its face against the juvenile death penalty."

The Court's Reasoning

On the basis of these three amorphous inquiries, the court set aside the death sentence in the case before it, as well as the application of all state laws allowing similar punishment.

Since that decision, "human rights" organizations and juvenile-criminal advocates have turned their sights to life without parole for juvenile offenders, arguing that, based on *Roper*'s reasoning, it should be next on the court's Eighth Amendment chopping block. In their speeches, reports, and briefs, they claim that this is the next logical step in the evolution of the law and that the death penalty and life without parole, which they frequently refer to as a "death sentence," are perfectly analogous.

Nothing in *Roper*, however, supports those pat conclusions. Quite the opposite: *Roper* undercuts their case. Rhetorical comparisons aside, all three of the factors that mitigated against the juvenile death penalty in *Roper* support continued application of life without parole for juvenile offenders.

Support for Juvenile Life Without Parole

First, "objective indicia" demonstrate a "national consensus" in support of life without parole for juvenile offenders. The raw numbers are overwhelming: 43 states, the federal government, and the District of Columbia allow life without parole for juvenile offenders; only seven states forbid it. Of those 44 (the 43 states and D.C.), only five could be "knocked out" because in practice they employ the sentence only rarely or not at all.

By this initial measure, then, 86 percent of states, containing over 90 percent of the national population, have and use life without parole for juvenile offenders. Further, in 26 of those states, life without parole is the mandatory sentence for anyone—adult or juvenile—convicted of first-degree murder, evincing the states' comfort in applying this sentence to the most serious offenders.

Data on the trend in state laws point in the same direction. Since the 1980s, states have gotten tough on juvenile crime, passing many laws allowing for the automatic transfer of juvenile offenders from the juvenile justice system into regular criminal courts. Only 14 states had such laws in place in 1979, but by 2003, the number had reached 31, with an additional 14 states allowing prosecutors to decide whether to file charges in juvenile or criminal court. At the same time, many states have reduced the age at which juvenile court jurisdiction ends and have expanded the scope, specified in age and by offense, of automatic transfer statutes. The result is that a larger proportion of juvenile offenders than ever before are now subject to adult courts and adult punishment, including life without parole, sometimes as a mandatory sentence.

The unsurprising result of this legislative activity is that more juveniles are receiving sentences of life without parole. Even opponents of life sentences for juvenile offenders acknowledge that use of this sentencing tool is on the rise. A 2008 University of San Francisco report, for example, estimates that "the rate at which states sentence minors to life without parole remains at least three times higher than it was 15 years ago." The same report states that "the sentence was rarely imposed until the 1990s," providing a strong indication of the strength of the trend in favor of life sentences for juvenile offenders.

Against this trend stand two states: Colorado, which changed its parole statute in 2006 to allow those who are sentenced to life for offenses committed while under the age of 18 to seek parole after serving 40 years, and Montana, which in 2007 abrogated restrictions on parole eligibility for a half-dozen classes of offenders, including juveniles. Meanwhile, at least six state legislatures, as well as the U.S. Congress, have considered but declined to pass legislation to eliminate or restrict the sentence.

So there is a national consensus on life without parole for juvenile offenders. The same objective indicia considered in *Roper* show that this consensus is overwhelmingly in favor of it.

The Difference Between Life and Death

Roper's second factor, "the court's own determination in the exercise of its independent judgment," would be difficult to apply were it not for the fact that the court has already undertaken the analysis. While its findings on the culpability of juveniles could be seen as applying against life sentences, the court was clear that its analysis applies only to capital sentencing.

This makes logical sense: The court simply concluded that since juveniles could not possibly be within the class of "the worst offenders," sentencing them to death would necessarily violate its requirement that death be limited to the narrow category of offenders whose "extreme culpability makes them the most deserving of execution." Juveniles cannot be among the worst, reasoned the court, because the death penalty's marginal deterrent effect is vanishingly small relative to "life imprisonment without the possibility of parole . . . itself a severe sanction, in particular for a young person." Thus, the court's determination of its "independent judgment" in *Roper* rests on the continued availability of life without parole for juvenile offenders.

Third, the international "unanimity" in which the court found solace in *Roper* simply does not exist for life-without-parole sentences. The sentence is available in at least 11 countries, including Australia, and most of those countries share America's common-law heritage. Further, a multitude of countries allow sentences of long durations for juvenile offenders, which in some instances may be the practical equivalent of life without parole. Other countries, meanwhile, have agreed to prohibit the sentence but have not done so in practice.

Thus, the "weight of international opinion" in common-law countries is mixed and far lighter overall than in the case of the death penalty. And as the court acknowledges, even very weighty evidence of foreign practices does not control U.S. law and can provide only "significant confirmation" of the court's judgments under U.S. law.

The two primary factors in *Roper*—national consensus and the court's own judgment—preclude the same result as *Roper* in the life-without-parole context, assuming that the court is even willing to take the unprecedented step of expanding the reach of its death jurisprudence. It is far more likely that the court would hew to its "narrow proportionality" line, never moving beyond the initial inquiry: *viz* [namely], whether the penalty is grossly disproportionate to the crime.

Any other result would require the court to radically revise the entirety of its Eighth Amendment jurisprudence as concerns both capital and noncapital offenses, throwing the entire nation's criminal justice system into chaos. Even a more activist court that was less divided over the question in *Roper* would balk at that prospect.

"*LWOP [life without parole] sentences are costly, shortsighted, and ignore the potential for transformative personal growth.*"

Life-Without-Parole Sentences Should Be Eliminated

Ashley Nellis

In the following viewpoint, Ashley Nellis argues that sentences of life without parole should be terminated. Nellis claims that such sentences show a disturbing distrust of the justice system and a troubling desire to incapacitate offenders and exact revenge. She contends that the marked increase in life-without-parole sentences over the last few decades is costly and ignores the possibility that prisoners can be rehabilitated. Nellis is a research analyst with the Sentencing Project, a national organization that promotes reforms in sentencing law and practice, as well as alternatives to incarceration.

As you read, consider the following questions:

1. According to Nellis, the number of people serving a life-without-parole sentence has increased by a factor of what between 1992 and 2008?

Ashley Nellis, "Throwing Away the Key: The Expansion of Life Without Parole Sentences in the United States," *Federal Sentencing Reporter*, vol. 23, no. 1, pp. 27–30. Copyright © 2010 by the University of California Press. All rights reserved. Reproduced by permission.

2. The author points to a 2004 analysis finding that people released from life sentences were how much less likely to be rearrested within three years than other released individuals?

3. Nellis contends that according to an analysis of California inmates, incarcerating inmates over fifty-five years of age is how much more costly than those under fifty-five?

A mong the 1.6 million people incarcerated in U.S. prisons lives a rising population of people who will spend the remainder of their natural lives there because they have received a sentence of life without parole (LWOP). The rising number of LWOP prisoners is the end result of three decades of tough-on-crime policies that have made little impact on crime but have had profound consequences for American society.

A Change in Sentencing

Changes in crime policies over the past few decades have been wide ranging and include such features as an increased emphasis on drug enforcement and determinate sentences and, most significantly, a vastly expanded use of imprisonment. Simultaneously, diminishing value has been placed on the principle of rehabilitation that once guided the nation's correctional philosophy, however flawed it may have been in its implementation.

Foremost among the changes affecting the prison population in recent years are laws and policies regarding the expansion of LWOP sentences. Today 140,610 individuals—one of every eleven individuals in prison—are serving life sentences and just over 29 percent of them (41,095) will never be eligible for parole. The number of individuals serving life-without-parole sentences increased roughly 22 percent between 2003 and 2008, from 33,633 to 41,095, nearly four times the rate of growth of the parole-eligible life sentenced population.

Even though various types of life sentences have existed for a long time in the United States, they were generally indeterminate, with the possibility of parole to serve as an incentive for self-improvement. Over the past few decades, some notable changes have made life sentences more common. First, legislators have dramatically expanded the types of offenses that result in a parole-ineligible life sentence. Second, policy makers have established a wide range of habitual offender laws that subject a growing proportion of defendants to potential life terms of incarceration with no chance for parole. Finally, prison terms that extend beyond the expected life span (e.g., 90 years) are far more common today than twenty years ago. Combined, these changes help to explain the rise in life sentences among U.S. prisoners.

Sentencing considerations for individuals who have been convicted of serious acts of violence will clearly focus on goals of punishment and incapacitation. For individuals who have taken lives or who pose a serious threat to public safety, incapacitation as a means of ensuring public safety is a legitimate and compelling concern at sentencing. Yet, the issue of parole-ineligible life sentences is far more complex and cannot be regarded as merely strict sentencing for a deserving population of individuals convicted of serious offenses.

As discussed subsequently, the expanding use of LWOP sentences reflects a loss of confidence in personal reformation, which guided prison reforms as far back as the late 1800s, in favor of a misguided preference for retribution. It also rejects the view that individuals who commit crimes—even serious crimes—often mature out of their criminal behavior and become a reduced threat to public safety over time, despite social science, medical, and behavioral research that has reliably established this outcome. Knowledge of this fact leads one to question the rationale behind incarcerating those who present a minimal crime risk at the expense of a high tax burden on the public.

The Increasing Use of LWOP Sentences

In 2008, 41,095 people, or one in thirty-nine individuals in prison, were serving a sentence of life without parole. Most LWOP prisoners are male; women comprise slightly more than 3 percent of this group (1,333). The number of people serving LWOP has increased dramatically in recent years. In 1992, 12,453 individuals—one in sixty-eight—were serving LWOP sentences. In the intervening sixteen years, that figure has tripled.

Although most individuals serving LWOP sentences have been convicted of murder, depending on state law, LWOP can be used for a variety of offenses. In at least 37 states, LWOP is available for non-homicide convictions, including convictions for kidnapping, burglary, robbery, carjacking, and battery. LWOP is mandatory in many states upon a murder conviction, but in other states—such as Alabama, California, Florida, Georgia, Louisiana, South Carolina, Virginia, and Washington—LWOP is mandatory upon conviction of serious habitual offender laws. Under Florida's Prison Releasee Reoffender law, for instance, the state requires the mandatory maximum sentence upon conviction of a serious crime if it occurs after release from prison within the previous three years. In 2010, a 22-year-old defendant convicted of robbing a sandwich shop received an LWOP sentence under this law as a result of his having been released from prison for a previous drug conviction.

In six states—Illinois, Iowa, Louisiana, Maine, Pennsylvania, and South Dakota—and in the federal system, all life sentences are imposed without the possibility of parole. Only Alaska provides the possibility of parole for all life sentences, whereas the remaining forty-three states have laws that permit sentencing defendants to life with or without parole. In twenty-seven states, LWOP is mandatory upon conviction of at least one specified offense.

In Louisiana, where all life sentences lack the possibility of parole, one of every nine (10.9 percent) people in prison is serving an LWOP sentence. Pennsylvania, another LWOP-only state, incarcerates 9.4 percent of its prison population for the rest of their lives. Nationally, there are nine states in which more than 5 percent of individuals in prison are serving an LWOP sentence. On the other end of the spectrum, there are fifteen states in which less than 1 percent of prisoners are serving LWOP sentences.

It has long been recognized that racial disparities permeate the justice system, from the point of contact with law enforcement through sentencing and incarceration. Prison sentences tend to be more likely, as well as lengthier, for African Americans as compared with whites. Keeping with this pattern, people of color also represent a disproportionate share of LWOP sentences. Overall, blacks comprise 56.4 percent of the LWOP population; state-level analysis shows that in some states, the proportion of blacks serving LWOP sentences is as high as 73.3 percent, as is the case in Louisiana. In the federal system, 877 (71.3%) of the 1,230 LWOP prisoners are African American.

A Lack of Trust

A number of recurring themes emerge among the debates surrounding the use of LWOP. The main justifications typically offered for LWOP sentences center on distrust of the criminal justice system, a lack of confidence that offenders can reform their lives, and a powerful desire to punish. Yet, these justifications must be considered in the light of strong evidence that LWOP sentences impose unnecessary costs on the public, deny this population of prisoners the opportunity to demonstrate that they have reformed their lives, and do not necessarily keep the public safer.

Support for the expansion of LWOP sentences grew out of the same lack of trust in the judicial process that led to determinate sentencing, mandatory minimums, and truth-in-sentencing laws that restrict parole eligibility. Mounting public dissatisfaction with the justice system, particularly in the late 1980s and 1990s, was part of a larger movement toward more legislative control of the criminal justice process at the expense of the discretion of judges and parole boards. The overarching sentiment was that the system was broken. The expansion of LWOP sentencing and enhanced restrictions on parole-eligible life sentences were intended to ensure that life means life.

LWOP and other excessively harsh sentences have often been politically inspired and fueled by sensationalized accounts of people sentenced to life, often for violent crimes, who were released on parole after what was perceived to be too short a period in prison. A recent demonstration is the case of Maurice Clemmons, a convicted felon with an unusually long and violent criminal career that ended with the murder of four law enforcement officers in Parkland, Washington, in late 2009.

A case like Clemmons's is quite disturbing, but also quite rare; this case was riddled with missteps by criminal justice practitioners in their response to his violence over the years. Yet such cases attract media attention, instill fear in the public, and are often cited by legislators in order to garner support for tougher sentencing laws. Crime policies should not be based on rare events that, although tragic, do not reflect the typical behaviors of the people who leave prison.

A Long Sentence vs. a Life Sentence

The incentive to incapacitate rather than rehabilitate is also driven by a lack of confidence in offenders' ability or willingness to turn their lives around. The assumption with this line of thinking is that those who commit crimes—especially serious crimes—will repeat their illegal behavior once given the opportunity, thus making incapacitation the ideal choice.

Life Without Parole (LWOP) Sentences, 2008

State	LWOP	State	LWOP
Alabama	1,413	Montana	51
Alaska	na	Nebraska	213
Arizona	208	Nevada	450
Arkansas	541	New Hampshire	63
California	3,679	New Jersey	46
Colorado	464	New Mexico	0
Connecticut	334	New York	190
Delaware	318	North Carolina	1,215
Florida	6,424	North Dakota	11
Georgia	486	Ohio	216
Hawaii	47	Oklahoma	623
Idaho	102	Oregon	143
Illinois[a]	103	Pennsylvania	4,343
Indiana	96	Rhode Island	32
Iowa	616	South Carolina	777
Kansas	2	South Dakota	169
Kentucky	66	Tennessee	260
Louisiana	4,161	Texas	71
Maine	54	Utah	unknown
Maryland	321	Vermont	13
Massachusetts	902	Virginia	774
Michigan	3,384	Washington	542
Minnesota	48	West Virginia	251
Mississippi	1,230	Wisconsin	171
Missouri	938	Wyoming	20
		FEDERAL	4,514
		TOTALS	41,095

[a] Illinois did not provide usable data on life sentences or LWOP sentences in 2008. In 2003, the year in which data were previously collected for The Sentencing Project's report, *The Meaning of Life*, Illinois reported 233 individuals serving life sentences, 66 of which were LWOP. The prison population reported at this time was 2,589. Included in this table are 103 juvenile LWOP prisoners, confirmed through an independent report in 2008. The current number of adult life sentences and LWOP sentences in Illinois could not be determined.

TAKEN FROM: Ashley Nellis, "Throwing Away the Key: The Expansion of Life Without Parole Sentences in the United States," *Federal Sentencing Reporter*, vol. 23, no. 1, October 2010.

However, lifers are uniquely situated to desist from crime upon release because of the duration of their imprisonment, the maturity they are likely to gain in prison, and their age upon reentry into the community. For these reasons, recidivism rates are low among older inmates, including lifers, who are released. Unfortunately, a popular belief is that once sent to prison, a person should be ineligible for another chance at a law-abiding life.

Prisoners who serve a substantial period of time in prison after committing a serious crime generally have a diminished likelihood of reoffending. A difference between a long sentence (e.g., fifteen years) and a life sentence in terms of public safety has not been established, yet the cost difference between the two sentences is quite large, forcing taxpayers to bear the burden of housing those who pose minimal public safety risks.

The Issue of Recidivism

Recidivism rates for individuals serving a life sentence are considerably lower than for the general released prison population. A 2004 analysis found that individuals who were released from a life sentence were less than one-third as likely to be rearrested within three years as all released individuals. Whereas two-thirds of all individuals released in 1994 were rearrested within three years, only one-fifth of those released from a life sentence were rearrested.

Other research confirms the low recidivism rate of offenders who serve long sentences. Although not specifically addressing recidivism rates for individuals sentenced to life, a study in Ohio of twenty-one people released in 2000 who were 50 years of age or older and had served twenty-five years or more at the time of release found that none of these individuals committed a new crime during the three years after their release. In Pennsylvania, the recidivism rate of individuals convicted of new offenses who were 50 years of age or older and released in 2003 was 1.4 percent in the first twenty-two months after release. Although Pennsylvania does not permit parole for individuals convicted of a life sentence, research on 285 individuals who had their life sentences commuted and were released from prison found a recidivism rate for a new criminal conviction of just 1 percent.

These studies do not evaluate life sentences directly, but they are drawn from a similarly situated population, such as older people who have served upwards of twenty years in prison. Thus, they are illustrative of likely outcomes among individuals who have been sentenced to life should they be released. In fact, the research literature is replete with support for the perspective that individuals serving a life sentence are some of the most well-adjusted individuals in prison. For these individuals, prison becomes their social universe for the long term, and maintaining order becomes a priority. Whereas the assumption is that life-sentenced individuals with nothing to lose will be the most difficult population to manage, individuals serving a life sentence in fact are frequently lauded by correctional administrators as easy to manage. For instance, Alabama officials reported that LWOP inmates are half as likely to commit disciplinary offenses as other inmates.

The Desire for Retribution

Another justification for the use of LWOP is to exact revenge for harms done. Especially in more recent times, policy makers and the public have favored overly punitive and often irrational crime policies, usually derived from fear. Too often, these policies appear to be driven by political motivations to sound tough on crime. It is not difficult to find statements from elected officials such as the following, issued by a former assistant attorney general from Alabama [Edward Carnes]: "[L]ife without parole in Alabama means just that—no parole, no commutation, no way out until the day you die, period."

Yet practitioners frequently note the excessively harsh penalties that are required by some of these policies. In a review of federal judges' opinions on sentencing, repeated concern was voiced about extremely long sentences for nonviolent and first-time offenders. According to one judge, sentences that held nonviolent offenders past the age of 60 years old were "pointless." Moreover, some judges were troubled that, with no likelihood of release before death or old age, these defendants would have no hope and, therefore, little incentive to be model prisoners. A good number of federal judges, self-identified as Republicans, also remarked on the financial carelessness of LWOP and other excessive sentences. They noted that to give "thirty years when fifteen would accomplish the same goal does not make sense to appointees from a party which preaches fiscal conservatism and reduced federal spending" [quoted in David M. Zlotnick, "The Future of Federal Sentencing Policy: Learning Lessons from Republican Judicial Appointees in the Guidelines Era," *University of Colorado Law Review*, 2008].

Federal judges have expressed much frustration with their limited discretion at the sentencing stage. Even individuals who pose little threat of physical harm are nevertheless subjected to LWOP sentences under harsh federal sentencing structures; often, these offenses are drug related. At the sentencing hearing for one case, a federal judge [Ronald Longstaff] remarked to the defendant: "The mandatory life sentence as applied to you is not just, it's an unfair sentence, and I find it very distasteful to have to impose it." The judge stated elsewhere that in this particular case he would have sentenced the defendant to ten to twelve years had he the discretion to do so.

Parole and earned sentence reductions can serve as an incentive for reform and a measure of a prisoner's suitability to be returned to society. Historically, life sentences were seen as indeterminate, with the possibility of parole as a catalyst for personal reflection and growth. The widespread decline in considering parole, even in cases of clearly demonstrated personal change, undermines the incentive for reform and sends a message to individuals in prison that any attempt at self-improvement will not be acknowledged. Even when LWOP prisoners seek self-improvement, they are often denied enrollment for prison programming because their self-improvement is not considered a priority.

Although concerns about public safety may fade as an individual ages in prison and becomes less of a threat, the rationale for punishment and retribution, frequently linked to the heinousness of the crime, does not diminish at nearly the same rate. In the case of many, the decision to deny the opportunity for parole is grounded in the retributive desire to continue to punish based on the details of the crime.

The Cost of Life Sentences

Imprisonment for the remainder of one's life with no hope for even a review of one's case raises a number of ethical and practical concerns. Some important considerations discussed in this section include the exorbitant costs of incarceration . . . and the international perspective on this practice.

The aging prison population that is in part a function of life sentences is of concern due to declining health and higher health care costs. Older individuals in prison frequently exhibited higher rates of health problems than the general population when they were originally sentenced to prison. This poorer health is the result of a number of factors, including higher rates of substance abuse and physical abuse and less access to health care. Higher rates of incarceration among individuals from low-income communities of color mean that disparities in overall health are elevated for the incarcerated population and magnified further among older, incarcerated individuals. The cumulative effect of an unhealthy lifestyle coupled with a prison environment that is not conducive to healthy living accelerates health problems among aging prisoners. This effect is particularly pronounced in the population of individuals over the age of 50.

Older prisoners are substantially more expensive to incarcerate. Higher rates of chronic illness among individuals over the age of 50 result in an increased frequency of medical visits, procedures, and dispensed medication. In one facility in Pennsylvania, estimated costs for prisoners receiving long-term care total $63,500 per year of incarceration. Analyses of California inmates have estimated that the cost of incarcerating an inmate who is 55 years old or older is three times higher than the cost of incarcerating someone under 55.

As the number of individuals serving LWOP sentences rises, costs also rise. An estimate by the Sentencing Project found that a state will spend upwards of $1 million to incarcerate a life-sentenced person for forty years (from age 30 through 70). Unsurprisingly, the intersection of increasing health care costs and a rapidly aging prison population has placed an enormous burden on corrections systems to pay for these required services. In no state has this struggle been starker than in California, where the correctional system is under federal receivership and has recently been ordered to cut the current prison population by as much as 40,000 prisoners. . . .

In many other industrialized nations, serious offenders are typically released after a maximum prison term of no more than thirty years. For instance, in Spain and Canada, the longest sentence an offender can receive is twenty-five or thirty years. In Germany, France, and Italy, LWOP has been declared unconstitutional. In the United Kingdom, it is allowable, but used quite sparingly; according to a recent estimate, only twenty-three inmates were serving this sentence. In Sweden, parole-ineligible life sentences are permissible, but never mandatory. The Council of Europe stated in 1977 that "it is inhuman to imprison a person for life without the hope of release," and that it would "be compatible neither with the modern principles on the treatment of prisoners . . . nor with the idea of the reintegration of offenders into society."

A More Sensible Response to Serious Crime

Those who support eliminating LWOP sentences on moral or practical grounds do not view the abolition of LWOP as a guaranteed release from prison. A parole-eligible life sentence does not give prisoners the *right* to be released, merely the opportunity for review at a reasonable point in their sentence. Case-by-case review of a variety of pertinent factors, conducted by a professional parole board, will allow for the release of those prisoners who no longer need to be incarcerated and the continued incarceration of those who do.

LWOP sentences are costly, shortsighted, and ignore the potential for transformative personal growth. The forty-nine states that allow LWOP—and among these, the six states and the federal system with LWOP-only sentences—should replace this structure with parole-eligible terms. An example may come from Canada, where all individuals serving life sentences are considered for parole after serving ten to twenty-five years.

Again, such a change would not necessarily mean that all parole-eligible individuals would be released at some point during their term. In the interest of public safety, many individuals sentenced to life will serve the remainder of their natural lives in prison. However, this reform would delegate that decision to those who could periodically review prison sentences and prisoner progress since entering prison, taking into account a person's prospects for a successful transition to the community.

| "The basic reform is to substitute swift-
ness and certainty for severity."

Swift and Certain Punishment Works Better than Severe Sentences

Mark Kleiman, as told to Zach Weissmueller

In the following viewpoint, Zach Weissmueller interviews Mark Kleiman. Kleiman contends that the US criminal justice system punishes criminals too randomly and too severely. Kleiman advocates reform to the criminal justice system that enforces the law through definite, quick punishment that is less severe. He contends that such reform would work best to deter criminals and decrease the crime rate. Weissmueller is associate producer of ReasonTV, a project of the Reason Foundation. Kleiman is a professor of public policy at the Luskin School of Public Affairs at the University of California, Los Angeles.

As you read, consider the following questions:

1. According to Kleiman, although the United States has only 5 percent of the world's population, it has what percentage of the world's prisoners?

Zach Weissmueller, "'Long Prison Terms Are Wasteful Government Spending': Criminologist Mark Kleiman on Replacing Severity with Swiftness and Certainty," *Reason*, July 2011. Copyright © 2011 by The Reason Foundation. All rights reserved. Reproduced by permission.

2. Kleiman claims that a severe punishment can't be swift for what reason?

3. According to the viewpoint, what have American voters consistently wanted since the crime movement in the 1960s?

UCLA [University of California, Los Angeles] criminologist Mark Kleiman says he's "angry about having much too much crime and an intolerable number of people behind bars." Kleiman believes America's astronomical incarceration rate isn't making us safer. In his recent book *When Brute Force Fails: How to Have Less Crime and Less Punishment* (Princeton University Press), he argues that when it comes to punishment, there is a trade-off between severity and swiftness. For too long the U.S. has erred heavily on the side of severity, he says, but concentrating enforcement and providing immediate consequences for lawbreakers can reduce crime while putting fewer people in prison.

ReasonTV's Zach Weissmueller spoke with Kleiman late last year [2010]. . . .

America's Criminal Justice System

Weissmueller: What motivated you to write this book?

Mark Kleiman: I wrote *When Brute Force Fails* because I'm both excited and angry. I'm angry about having much too much crime and an intolerable number of people behind bars, and excited because out in the field people are doing things that could change that.

There are more people behind bars in the United States than in any other country in the world. We have more prisoners than China does. We have 5 percent of the world's population; we have 25 percent of the world's prisoners. If the criminal justice system were a parent, we'd call it abusive and neglectful. It punishes too much and not often enough. We have a criminal justice system that does not know what every competent parent knows: that you change people's behavior by giving them clear rules and by enforcing those rules consistently and quickly and fairly.

The Problem of Random Severity

What are the main reforms you're suggesting?

The worst thing about our criminal justice system is its randomized draconianism. We're very severe in the way we punish people, but we do so very irregularly and very erratically. The basic reform is to substitute swiftness and certainty for severity.

The average probation violation leads to no punishment at all, but an occasional probation violation will lead to six months in prison. That's the best possible way to fill up your prisons and not change anyone's behavior. The typical probation department does drug testing and tells people that they're not supposed to use. If the test comes back positive, the probation officer says, "Don't do that again." The next time it happens, the probation officer says, "Don't do that again." The third time, the probation officer says, "You know, if you keep doing this, you're going to get in trouble." The fourth time, he says, "This is your last warning." And about the eighth or ninth or 12th time, they're seeing the judge, and the probationer might be off to prison for six months. Lunacy. He had no way of knowing that the last "last warning" was really the last warning.

Prioritizing Swiftness over Severity

In the book, you say, "Concentrating enforcement attention works better than dispersing it." Explain what you mean.

If you've got a large number of violations and can't punish all of them, there are two approaches: You can punish more or less at random, in which case everybody learns that mostly he's going to get away with it. Or you can pick some subset of offenders, of offenses, of locations, of times—pick some part of the universe—and say, "OK, here's the rule within that part of the universe." Concentrated enforcement means deciding what you're not going to tolerate and who you're not going to tolerate doing it, directly communicating that threat to the people whose behavior you want to change, and then carrying it out.

You advocate a system that favors swiftness over severity. Why?

If offenders were perfectly rational, crime control would be easy: ratchet up the severity of the punishment to the point where even a small probability of being caught means it's not worth it. That's what we've been trying for the last 30 years, and it basically hasn't worked. Everybody is more sensitive to immediate consequences than to future consequences. Everybody is more sensitive to certain than to uncertain consequences. Offenders are probably more like that than the rest of us: They're more reckless; they're more impulsive. Therefore it's even more important to move the consequences close in time to the events and to have the link be highly probable.

You also say there's a trade-off between swiftness and severity.

We've known for a long time that swiftness and certainty are more important than severity. What's not adequately understood is that severity is the enemy of swiftness and certainty. A severe punishment can't be swift because there's a lot of due process involved, and it can't be certain, because you're chewing up a lot of resources. . . . It's a little strange that the people who are loudest about opposing wasteful government spending haven't noticed that long prison terms are wasteful government spending.

The Need for Vengeance

You describe a tension between safety and vengeance, results and catharsis. What do you say to people who argue that vengeance is an important part of justice?

I agree that vengeance is an important part of justice. The tone deafness of official criminology and the academy to the need for vengeance, it seems to me, has contributed to the problem. If you acknowledge the need for vengeance, then you can say "but it ought to be proportional."

The resistance to using DNA testing to find out whether somebody is guilty comes from prosecutors, the cops, and the victims—not all of them, but often enough. The psychological mechanism is clear. From the victim's point of view, what matters is that somebody was punished for that crime. But it ought to matter a little bit whether it was the right person.

The High Rate of Incarceration

What about critics who point out that crime rates have dropped, especially since the 1990s? Does this mean incarceration works?

Of course our high rate of incarceration to some extent must work, because people who are in prison aren't committing crimes on the outside. Now, if we counted the crime rate inside prisons, the crime drop would not have been as dramatic. I was a strong advocate of building more prisons, back when we had fewer than half a million prison cells. The first additional half million was well worth doing; the next million and a half, not so much. We made do with a fifth as many prisons as we have now. Everyone else in the world does that. We ought to figure out how to do that.

As [Justice Fellowship president] Pat Nolan says, right now we're imprisoning a lot of people we're mad at. We only ought to imprison people we're afraid of. There are three groups of people who ought to be in prison. There are people who do such appalling stuff that we want to make an example of them—say, [imprisoned defrauder] Bernie Madoff. There are people who are violent criminals and whose rate of crime is high enough that it's worth $40,000 a year not to have them in our hair. And then there are people who won't behave on the outside. You put an ankle bracelet on him, he takes the ankle bracelet off; he's picked himself a prison cell. Everybody else we can adequately punish and control in the community.

Why do you think the justice system has evolved (or devolved) into an exercise in brute force?

The key thing about the American system is that we have police chiefs who are appointed by elected mayors and prosecutors who are themselves elected officials. They are very sensitive to what the voters want. And what the voters have wanted ever since the crime movement in the 1960s is revenge on the criminals. In some ways, I think voters were right to say, "Hey, crime's a big problem. We should do something about it." Unfortunately, they were badly misled by their politicians into thinking that random severity was a good solution.

| "There is virtually no data that is capable of demonstrating a direct link between federal mandatory penalties in particular and any declines in crime."

Mandatory Minimum Sentences Are Ineffective

Marc Mauer

In the following viewpoint, Marc Mauer argues that there is no evidence that federal mandatory penalties have increased public safety and that the decline in crime rates and rise in incarceration over the last few decades do not clearly have a causal relationship. Furthermore, Mauer contends that there is some evidence that mandatory minimum sentences may have an adverse effect on recidivism and reentry for drug offenders. Mauer is executive director of the Sentencing Project, a national organization that promotes reforms in sentencing law and practice, as well as alternatives to incarceration.

As you read, consider the following questions:

1. According to Mauer, the federal court system handles what fraction of all criminal cases?

Marc Mauer, "The Impact of Mandatory Minimum Penalties in Federal Sentencing," *Judicature*, vol. 94, no. 1, July/August 2010, pp. 6–7. Copyright © 2010 by the American Bar Association. All rights reserved. Reproduced by permission.

2. According to the author, what country experienced a crime decline in the 1990s along with a declining prison population?

3. The number of persons incarcerated for a drug offense has increased by what percentage since 1980, according to Mauer?

Mandatory minimum penalties have been enacted over time for a variety of reasons. Foremost among these are legislators' professed belief that such penalties will bring greater certainty to the sentencing process and that they will "send a message" to potential offenders that specified behaviors will be met with harsh and certain punishment.

The Effect of Federal Mandatory Penalties

Looking at the experience of the past several decades, some observers have contended that mandatory minimums, including such federal penalties, have produced significant benefits in reducing crime. At a 2009 congressional hearing, for example, former U.S. attorney Michael J. Sullivan asked, "Has the role that Congress played in sentencing, including the passage of mandatory minimum sentences, had an impact on public safety and crime?" He concluded that "the answer to that question can easily be found in crime statistics and is buttressed by anecdotal story after story from across our nation. Crime rates over the past 30 years certainly paint a picture of continuing success of reducing crime and victimization through sound public policy."

What, then, do we know about the extent to which federal mandatory penalties have been responsible for declines in crime? To date, there is virtually no data that is capable of demonstrating a direct link between federal mandatory penalties in particular and any declines in crime. Further, a broad range of research suggests that it is quite unlikely that these penalties would have such an impact.

In examining the effect of federal mandatory penalties, the key data problem is that the federal court system handles only a small fraction, less than 10 percent, of all criminal cases. Therefore, attempting to draw any conclusions about the specific impact of *federal mandatory penalties* on crime rates is fraught with imprecision. To state that the adoption of such penalties by Congress in the 1980s was directly responsible for reductions in a wide variety of crimes that are generally prosecuted in state courts requires a great leap of faith that is not supported by the evidence.

We can see this most clearly in the realm of drug offenses, the category in which federal mandatory penalties most often apply. Since drug offenses are widely prosecuted in both state and federal courts, a potential offender has no means of knowing in which court system he or she would be likely to be prosecuted (assuming, of course, that the offender is even thinking about the prospects of apprehension). Therefore, it is virtually impossible to break out any uniquely *federal* impact of mandatory sentencing.

The Impact on Crime Rates

Even aside from this problem, measuring the impact of harsh sentencing policies on crime rates is a complex undertaking. While it is the case that crime rates have generally been declining since the early 1990s and that this has taken place at a time when the prison population was rising, this does not necessarily suggest that there is a clear and unambiguous relationship between these two factors. Just prior to the beginnings of the crime decline, in the period 1984–91, incarceration rates increased substantially and yet crime rates increased as well.

Looking a bit more expansively, a comparison of trends in the U.S. and Canada in recent decades is instructive. While there has been a great deal of attention focused on the U.S. crime decline of the 1990s, similar declines were achieved in

Canada as well, yet these occurred while the prison population was actually declining. Thus, we should be exceedingly cautious in attributing any substantial causal effect between rising incarceration and declining crime rates.

While incarceration has some impact on crime, this effect is generally more modest than many believe. The most optimistic research to date on the crime decline of the 1990s finds that 25 percent of the decline in violent crime can be attributed to rising imprisonment, but other scholarly work concludes that this effect may be as small as 10 percent. And in either case, such studies do not tell us whether using resources to support expanded incarceration is *more* effective than targeted social interventions, such as expanded preschool programming, substance abuse treatment, or improving high school graduation rates, all of which have been demonstrated to improve public safety outcomes. Further, the rise in incarceration over the past two decades is a function of a range of factors, including increased drug arrests, harsher sentencing policies, reduced parole releases, and increased parole revocations. Federal mandatory sentencing penalties play a relatively small role in this overall scheme.

Mandatory Penalties for Drug Offenses

While there is little relevant data on the overall impact of federal mandatory penalties, there is nonetheless a broad range of evidence that suggests that it is unlikely that mandatory penalties for drug offenses have a significant impact on enhancing public safety. This is the case for several reasons:

Deterrence is primarily a function of the certainty, not severity, of punishment. To the extent that sentencing policies may deter individuals from engaging in crime, the research literature generally shows that increases in the certainty of punishment are much more likely to produce an effect than enhancements to the severity of punishment. That is, if we can increase the prospects that a given offender is apprehended,

The Goals of Deterrence and Incapacitation

Mandatory minimums may not fulfill consequentialist goals . . . by failing to provide effective, efficient deterrence or meaningful incapacitation. Clarity and certainty of punishment are not synonymous with deterrence, which requires that a defendant not only know the rule, but also believe that the costs outweigh the benefits from violating the law and then apply this understanding to decision making at the time of the crime. Most offenders neither perceive this balance of costs and benefits nor follow the rational actor model. In turn, incapacitation is only effective if: (1) the person imprisoned would otherwise commit crime, and (2) he is not replaced by others. Mandatory minimums prove problematic on both criteria. Offenders typically age out of the criminal lifestyle, with long obligatory sentences requiring the continued incarceration of individuals who would not be engaged in crime. Moreover, certain offenses subject to mandatory minimums can draw upon a large supply of potential participants; with drug organizations, for instance, an arrested dealer or courier is quickly replaced by another. It is not surprising, then, that most researchers reject crime-control arguments for mandatory sentencing laws.

Erik Luna, "Mandatory Minimum
Sentencing Provisions Under Federal Law,"
Testimony Before the United States Sentencing Commission,
May 27, 2010.

some persons will be deterred by that knowledge. But merely extending the amount of punishment that will be imposed, when most offenders don't believe they will be apprehended, does little to add to any deterrent effect. In this regard, mandatory penalties increase severity, but have no direct impact on increasing certainty, and are therefore not likely to provide any significant additional deterrent effects.

Mandatory penalties are particularly ineffective in addressing drug crimes. While there is an ongoing debate about the effect of imprisonment on reducing crime, drug offenses are particularly immune to being affected by more and longer prison terms. This is largely due to the "replacement" nature of these offenses, the fact that there is a virtually endless supply of potential offenders in the drug trade. Since the vast majority of incarcerated drug offenders are from the lower and middle ranks of the drug trade, their imprisonment in effect creates a "job opportunity" for someone else seeking to earn some quick money. As long as there is a demand for illegal drugs, there will be a large pool of potential sellers, as evidenced by the fact that the number of persons incarcerated for a drug offense has increased by more than 1000 percent since 1980. Since federal mandatory penalties are disproportionately employed for drug offenses, this suggests that their overall impact is similarly limited.

Mandatory penalties may adversely affect recidivism. Whatever one may think about the wisdom of mandatory sentencing, it is undeniable that such penalties serve to increase the length of time that offenders serve in prison by restricting the discretion of judges and corrections/parole officials. By doing so, these policies may have a criminogenic effect. A 2002 review conducted by leading Canadian criminologists involved a meta-analysis of 117 studies measuring various aspects of recidivism. The researchers [Paula Smith, Claire Goggin, and Paul Gendreau] concluded that longer periods in prison were "associated with a small increase in recidivism" and that "the results appear to give some credence to the prison as 'schools of crime' perspective."

Federal mandatory penalties increase the challenges for successful reentry. While not a problem exclusive to mandatory sentencing, the combination of expanded federal prosecution of drug offenses along with lengthier prison terms produced by mandatory penalties exacerbates the challenges of reentry. This is due to the fact that since federal prisoners can be housed anywhere in the country, many are in prisons far from their homes and are also serving long prison terms. This combination of circumstances contributes to eroding ties to family and community, the critical ingredients of successful reentry. . . .

In regard to mandatory sentencing, there is a broad consensus among legal organizations, scholars, and many practitioners that such policies are counterproductive to a fair and effective system of justice. . . . Eliminating mandatory sentencing from the federal court system would represent a significant step toward developing a more rational and fair system of sentencing.

Periodical and Internet Sources Bibliography

The following articles have been selected to supplement the diverse views presented in this chapter.

Andrew Cohen — "The Death Penalty: Why We Fight for Equal Justice," *Atlantic*, September 19, 2011.

Ray Fisman — "Going Down Swinging," *Slate*, March 20, 2008. www.slate.com.

Jonah Goldberg — "Why Death-Penalty Opponents Can't Win," *National Review Online*, September 23, 2011. www.nationalreview.com.

Naomi Harlin Goodno — "Career Criminals Targeted: The Verdict Is In, California's Three Strikes Law Proves Effective," *Journal of the Institute for the Advancement of Criminal Justice*, Summer 2007.

Karen Heller — "Life Terms for Juveniles?," *Philadelphia Inquirer*, July 18, 2010.

Wendy Kaminer — "Mandatory Sentences and Myths of Equal Justice," *Atlantic*, December 22, 2010.

Scott Lemieux — "Executed Until Proven Guilty," *American Prospect*, September 22, 2011.

Los Angeles Times — "Three-Strikes Law: A Big Error," August 19, 2010.

Marc Mauer — "Beyond the Fair Sentencing Act," *Nation*, December 27, 2010.

New York Times — "An Invitation to Overreach," September 28, 2011.

David Onek — "It's Time to Reform Three Strikes," *Calitics*, February 23, 2011. www.calitics.com.

OPPOSING
VIEWPOINTS®
SERIES

CHAPTER 4

What Rights Should Be a Part of the Criminal Justice System?

Chapter Preface

When individuals in the United States are accused of a crime, they are entitled to certain protections under the law before and during trial. Although not specifically mentioned in the US Constitution, the presumption of innocence has always been the cornerstone of the rights of the accused. Justice Edward D. White, writing the majority opinion for *Coffin v. United States* on March 4, 1895, explicitly noted the tradition, stating: "The principle that there is a presumption of innocence in favor of the accused is the undoubted law, axiomatic and elementary, and its enforcement lies at the foundation of the administration of our criminal law." The Bill of Rights provides for several constitutional protections for criminal defendants under the Fourth, Fifth, and Sixth Amendments. Over the years, the constitutional rights of criminal defendants have been explicated, refined, and expanded by laws and court decisions.

Under the Fourth Amendment to the US Constitution, individuals are protected against "unreasonable searches and seizures." If law enforcement violates this requirement and conducts an illegal search, any evidence acquired is not admissible at trial, under what has become known as the exclusionary rule. There are good-faith exceptions to this, but in general the accused have the right not to have evidence introduced at trial when such evidence was gained in an unconstitutional manner.

Under the Fifth Amendment, it is established that defendants may not "be compelled in any criminal case to be a witness against himself"; that is, accused individuals have the right to remain silent before and during trial. This stems from the principle of presumption of innocence, placing the burden on the prosecution to prove that the defendant is guilty. Also under the Fifth Amendment is the protection against double jeopardy, guaranteeing that no person shall "be subject for the same offense to be twice put in jeopardy of life or limb." This guarantees that a criminal will be brought to criminal court only once for an offense, even if he or she faces multiple charges (the only exception being when the defendant faces both state criminal charges and federal criminal charges).

Under the Sixth Amendment, the rights related to criminal prosecutions are established. The amendment sets forth the trial rights of criminal defendants.

> In all criminal prosecutions, the accused shall enjoy the right to a speedy and public trial, by an impartial jury of the State and district wherein the crime shall have been committed, which district shall have been previously ascertained by law, and to be informed of the nature and cause of the accusation; to be confronted with the witnesses against him; to have compulsory process for obtaining witnesses in his favor, and to have the Assistance of Counsel for his defence.

The rights delineated under this amendment spell out the conditions of a fair trial: the right to a swift trial; the right to a public trial; the right to trial by an impartial jury; the right to face witnesses in court rather than allow prosecutors to rely on hearsay; and the right to be represented by an attorney. The US Supreme Court has determined that the right to an attorney also includes the right to court-appointed representation for those who cannot afford to hire their own attorneys.

The rights of criminal defendants under the Fourth, Fifth, and Sixth Amendments continue to be interpreted and refined. Some of the controversial issues stemming from the guarantees of the Bill of Rights are discussed in the following chapter, including the development of Miranda rights stemming from the Fifth Amendment and the right to legal representation under the Sixth Amendment.

| *"Let us not write off so easily a simple police procedure that has helped protect American civil liberties for decades."*

Terrorist Suspects Should Have a Right to Miranda Warnings

America

In the following viewpoint, the editors of America *argue that Miranda rights are in jeopardy in response to terrorist threats. The authors claim that recent cases prove that offering Miranda rights to terrorist suspects does not diminish the ability to gain information. The authors caution that weakening Miranda rights would diminish the good reputation of the US criminal justice system.* America *is a weekly Catholic Jesuit magazine; its editorial board is made up of both Jesuit priests and brothers, as well as laypeople.*

As you read, consider the following questions:

1. According to *America*, in what year was a Miranda warning first used?

2. A US Supreme Court decision in 1984 offered what exception to Miranda rights, according to the authors?

America, "Read Him His Rights," June 7, 2010. Americamagazine.org. Copyright © 2010 by America Press, Inc. All rights reserved. Reproduced by permission.

3. The authors compare the Obama administration to what other presidential administration, in terms of powers claimed for the president?

Television police dramas are crowded with scenes in which the hardened detective pushes a suspect up against an alley wall and intones, "You have the right to remain silent. . . ." This is the familiar language of the so-called Miranda warning, used to ensure that people arrested in the United States have at least a minimal understanding of their rights when they are facing criminal prosecution, above all the right to "clam up" and "lawyer up." The warning obviously helps protect the rights of the suspect, but, worth remembering, it also clears the path for police to use at trial any incriminating information they gather during interrogation.

The Attempt to Diminish Miranda Rights

Since its first use after the U.S. Supreme Court decision in the case *Miranda v. Arizona* in 1966, the warning represents the first line of a criminal suspect's defense even as it stands as the last line of protection for U.S. civil liberties. The era of the police procedural drama on television helped familiarize the entire nation with *Miranda* and what it meant.

Now a different kind of television drama is contributing to efforts to water it down. This one tantalizes with easy resolutions of terrorist threats at the hands of brutal if effective operatives dispatched by murky government agencies. Call it the Jack Bauer [fictional character who is a member of a counterterrorist unit] effect. In the imagined landscape of the show *24*, the bad guys of course do not deserve the protection offered by *Miranda*, and the civil liberty it protects puts an unnecessary burden on investigators at the same time that it increases the threat to public safety.

That indictment of *Miranda* makes good TV drama, but it has little to do with events in the real world. In two nonfictional attempted terror strikes on U.S. soil, both terror suspects were properly Mirandized. The Christmas bomber, Umar Farouk Abdulmutallab, after initially exercising his right to remain silent, has become a veritable font of information about his training and the terror network that activated him. The similarly Mirandized Times Square bomber, Faisal Shahzad—a U.S. citizen, it should be remembered—has likewise been an eager source of information for U.S. anti-terror efforts. So which reality should we refer to when constructing public policy: Jack Bauer's fantasy land of suspended civil liberties and intelligence extracted by torture or the real-world experience of the interrogations of Shahzad and Abdulmutallab, which have yielded a bonanza of good information for anti-terror efforts?

The Obama Administration

Nonetheless Attorney General Eric Holder has begun sending up trial balloon proposals for updating *Miranda*. Following the arrest of Shahzad, he and the [President Barack] Obama administration were roundly criticized because arresting officers followed the law and informed Shazad of his rights. Now Holder claims to be interested in seeking "necessary flexibility" to gather information from terror suspects by having Congress rework the Miranda rules. The Obama administration appears poised to fix a problem terror investigators do not have by revisiting a premier element of a civil liberty that citizens of a mature democracy should be able to take for granted. Let's remember that a Supreme Court decision from 1984 already offers a public-safety exception to *Miranda*. Mr. Holder has said that the Obama administration will seek only to clarify that ruling—a commitment to which it must be firmly held if it cannot be dissuaded from messing with *Miranda* in the first place. [Editor's note: The Obama administration expanded exceptions to the public-safety rule for terrorist suspects in 2011.]

The Miranda Holding

When an individual is taken into custody or otherwise deprived of his freedom by the authorities in any significant way and is subjected to questioning, the privilege against self-incrimination is jeopardized. Procedural safeguards must be employed to protect the privilege, and unless other fully effective means are adopted to notify the person of his right of silence and to assure that the exercise of the right will be scrupulously honored, the following measures are required. He must be warned prior to any questioning that he has the right to remain silent, that anything he says can be used against him in a court of law, that he has the right to the presence of an attorney, and that, if he cannot afford an attorney one will be appointed for him prior to any questioning if he so desires. Opportunity to exercise these rights must be afforded to him throughout the interrogation. After such warnings have been given, and such opportunity afforded him, the individual may knowingly and intelligently waive these rights and agree to answer questions or make a statement. But unless and until such warnings and waiver are demonstrated by the prosecution at trial, no evidence obtained as a result of interrogation can be used against him.

Earl Warren, Majority Opinion,
Miranda v. Arizona, *June 13, 1966.*

As a candidate, the president often remarked that the nation need not surrender its cultural values in order to defeat global terror, but since assuming office he has adopted many of the extraordinary powers first claimed for the president in the [President George W.] Bush era. The Obama administration has continued or accelerated information-gathering techniques that have raised concerns among civil libertarians, and it now proposes to reconsider *Miranda*'s unique role in U.S. jurisprudence. How much weaker can we make *Miranda* before we diminish the liberty of all Americans in an effort to thwart those who threaten them?

Respect for the U.S. Legal System

We have already surrendered much, and perhaps more that we still do not know about, in the effort against global terror networks. But people all over the world still hold the American judicial system in high esteem. Part of the reason the parents of the failed Christmas bomber Abdulmutallab were so willing to cooperate in his interrogation—his father tipped off American officials about the possible threat from their son—was their high regard for the U.S. legal system and their confidence that their son would be treated fairly and humanely.

Let's not give them, and free people everywhere who may wish to assist the United States against terrorism in the future, reason to suspect that America is wavering in its commitment to fairness and the rule of law out of a desire to achieve maximum security. Let us not write off so easily a simple police procedure that has helped protect American civil liberties for decades.

> "The public-safety exception should be enlarged to allow law enforcement to interrogate, without Mirandizing, those arrested in the commission of terrorist crimes."

Terrorist Suspects Should Not Have a Right to Miranda Warnings

Charles Krauthammer

In the following viewpoint, Charles Krauthammer argues that the right to remain silent protected under the Miranda safeguards was never meant to apply to terrorist suspects. Krauthammer claims that giving terrorist suspects Miranda warnings jeopardizes national safety. Krauthammer prefers that terrorist suspects be put into military custody rather than tried in civilian courts. He concludes that if civilian courts are to be used, then the public-safety exception needs to be enlarged to allow law enforcement to interrogate terrorist suspects without giving Miranda warnings. Krauthammer is a nationally syndicated columnist.

As you read, consider the following questions:

1. According to Krauthammer, what did authorities do in order to obtain information from Faisal Shahzad, the confessed Times Square bomber?

2. What does Krauthammer imply is more important than gaining the conviction of a low-level terrorist?

3. Krauthammer claims that no Miranda warnings should be given to terrorist suspects until what happens?

"[Law enforcement] interviewed Mr. Shahzad ... under the public-safety exception to the Miranda *rule.... He was eventually ... Mirandized and continued talking."*

—John Pistole, FBI deputy director, May 4 [2010]

All well and good. But what if Faisal Shahzad, the confessed Times Square bomber, had *stopped* talking? When you tell someone he has the right to remain silent, there is a distinct possibility that he will remain silent, is there not? And then what?

The Public-Safety Exception

The authorities deserve full credit for capturing Shahzad within 54 hours. Credit is also due them for obtaining information from him by invoking the "public safety" exception to the *Miranda* rule.

But then Shahzad was Mirandized. If he had decided to shut up, it would have denied us valuable information—everything he is presumably telling us now about Pakistani contacts, training, plans for *other* possible plots beyond the Times Square attack.

The public-safety exception is sometimes called the "ticking-time-bomb" exception. But what about information regarding bombs not yet ticking but being planned and readied to kill later?

The Role of Miranda Warnings

Think of the reason why we give *any* suspect Miranda warnings. It is not that you're prohibited from asking questions before Mirandizing. You can ask a suspect anything you damn well please. You can ask him if he picks his feet in Poughkeepsie—but without Miranda warnings, the answers are not admissible in court.

In this case, however, Miranda warnings were superfluous. Shahzad had confessed to the car-bombing attempt while being interrogated under the public-safety exception. That's admissible evidence. Plus, he left a treasure trove of physical evidence all over the place—which is how we caught him in two days.

Second, even assuming that by not Mirandizing him we might have jeopardized our chances of getting some convictions—so what? Which is more important: (a) gaining, a year or two hence, the conviction of a pigeon—the last and now least important link in this terror chain—whom we could surely get off the street with explosives and weapons charges, or (b) preventing future terror attacks on Americans by learning from Shahzad what he might know about terror plots in Pakistan and sleeper cells in the United States?

Even posing this choice demonstrates why the very use of the civilian judicial system to interrogate terrorists is misconceived, even if they are, like Shahzad, (naturalized) American citizens. America is the target of an ongoing jihadist campaign. The logical and serious way to defend ourselves is to place captured terrorists in military custody as unlawful enemy combatants. As former anti-terror prosecutor Andrew McCarthy notes in *National Review*, one of the six World War II German saboteurs captured in the U.S., tried by military commission, and executed was a U.S. citizen. It made no difference.

Miranda Rights as a Trial Tool

Behind the government's use of *Miranda* is an underlying assumption: The case is going to trial, and the government wants to preserve the possibility of using the defendant's statements against him in its case. Thus, *Miranda* is a trial tool—not a national security tool.

Charles D. Stimson and James Jay Carafano,
"Treating Terrorism Solely as a Law Enforcement Matter—
Not Miranda—Is the Problem," Heritage Foundation,
May 13, 2010. www.heritage.org.

Miranda Rights for Terrorist Suspects

But let's assume you're wedded to the civilian-law-enforcement model, as the [President Barack] Obama administration is. At least make an attempt to expand the public-safety exception to *Miranda* in a way that takes into account the jihadist war that did not exist when that exception was narrowly drawn by the Supreme Court in the 1984 [*New York v.*] *Quarles* case.

The public-safety exception should be enlarged to allow law enforcement to interrogate, without Mirandizing, those arrested in the commission of terrorist crimes (and make the answers admissible)—until law enforcement is satisfied that vital intelligence related to other possible plots and threats to public safety has been sufficiently acquired.

This could be done by congressional statute. Or the administration could, in an actual case, refrain from Mirandizing until it had explored the outer limits of any plot—and then defend its actions before the courts, resting its argument on the Supreme Court's own logic in the *Quarles* case: "We conclude that the need for answers to questions in a situation posing a threat to the public safety outweighs the need for the

[*Miranda*] rule." [Editor's note: The Obama administration expanded exceptions to the public-safety rule for terrorist suspects in 2011.]

Otherwise, we will be left—when a terrorist shuts up, as did the underwear bomber [Umar Farouk Abdulmutallab] for five weeks—in the absurd position of capturing enemy combatants and then prohibiting ourselves from obtaining the information they have, and we need, to protect innocent lives.

My view is that we should treat enemy combatants as enemy combatants, whether they are U.S. citizens (Shahzad) or not (the underwear bomber). If, however, they are to be treated as ordinary criminals, then at least agree on this: no Miranda rights until we know everything that public safety demands we need to know.

"Court-appointed lawyers who don't meet—or even talk to—clients until the eve of trial are one symptom of a crumbling public defense system."

The Right to Adequate Legal Defense Is Not Being Met for the Poor

Vanessa Gregory

In the following viewpoint, Vanessa Gregory argues that those who cannot pay for legal representation—the poor—do not get adequate legal representation through the public defense system. Gregory claims that the public defense system, although it varies in each county, is generally underfunded, and public defenders are overworked. She concludes that the states need to do a better job of instituting and enforcing standards on the public defense system and that such efforts should be backed by the federal government. Gregory is a writer and teaches at the University of Mississippi's Meek School of Journalism and New Media.

As you read, consider the following questions:

1. What states are at the high end and low end of per-capita spending on public defense, according to a 2008 report cited by the author?

2. According to Gregory, what was the median starting salary for public defenders in 2007?

3. According to the author, the Department of Justice's Access to Justice Initiative is advising jurisdictions in what three states?

June Hardwick has been brainstorming with a black marker on poster-size papers covering her office wall. The Jackson, Mississippi, assistant public defender is reviewing the facts—and possible defense arguments—in a client's statutory rape case. "No rape kit," reads a bullet point. "No panties," reads another. She has stacked and sorted her indicted cases on the floor beneath the papers; each folder represents a person too poor to hire a private attorney. On top of the last pile sits a note on which Hardwick has scrawled "need to visit."

That Hardwick plans to see clients in jail shouldn't be re-markable. But court-appointed lawyers who don't meet—or even talk to—clients until the eve of trial are one symptom of a crumbling public defense system that critics say fails clients, communities, taxpayers, and the Constitution. In the worst instances of substandard legal defense, the innocent lose liberty. More commonly, a poor person serves extra time when robust counsel might have secured a shorter sentence, probation, or stint in a drug-rehabilitation program.

National numbers on indigent defense are scarce, but it's clear that the vast majority of defendants qualify for court-appointed counsel. Public defender offices across the U.S. spent $2.3 billion on more than 5 million cases in 2007—and those figures don't include expenditures in approximately 30 percent of counties, which use a contract or assigned-counsel system instead of staff attorneys. Of state and county public defense systems recently surveyed by the Bureau of Justice [Statistics], more than 70 percent reported caseloads that exceed national professional guidelines, a burden which can clog dockets and crowd jails before a verdict ever arrives.

After sentencing, there's the social cost of extra prison time and the actual cost: Incarcerating an inmate for a year averaged $22,650 in 2001, the latest year for which national data is available. More recent tallies, such as those from California, show skyrocketing costs. The Golden State spends nearly $50,000 a year to imprison an individual. Meanwhile, funding for indigent defense, which might minimize the prison population, is wildly uneven. According to a 2008 report from the National Legal Aid & Defender Association, per-capita spending on public defense ranges from $40.95 in Alaska to $4.15 in Mississippi, the lowest in the country.

Hardwick's office in Mississippi, like many across the country, has been further hamstrung by the recession: The Hinds County Board of Supervisors instituted furloughs one day a month for county employees in April. Despite this setback, Hardwick's ability to represent clients has improved thanks to the Southern Public Defender Training Center. The three-year classroom and mentorship program recruits and equips bright young lawyers to serve a corner of the justice system that desperately needs them. Lawyers attend two weeks of classes with veteran public defenders at Samford University's Cumberland School of Law in Birmingham, Alabama. They reconvene every six months to discuss challenges, consulting with mentors in the interim. The center has trained 95 attorneys since 2007. The neediest offices pay as little as $250 to enroll a public defender.

The center's founder, Atlanta lawyer Jonathan Rapping, says the program not only provides defense-specific education that's too expensive for many offices; it promotes professional pride and a culture of thorough, vigorous representation. "We need to have a community of public defenders who care as much about their clients as O.J. Simpson's lawyers cared about him," he says.

For Hardwick, who is in her second year of the program, the training has provided skills and experience that law school did not. She is learning strategies for persuading juries and communicating with clients. She has been encouraged to conduct her own investigations—a task she admits she hadn't been doing well. She has learned to excel in direct and cross-examinations and to break bad habits, like waiving preliminary hearings. "It's our first stab at discovery," Hardwick says. "Now I know how to milk it. I know how to ask all the questions that I need to help my client."

This year [2011], the Department of Justice awarded the Southern Public Defender Training Center a $700,000 grant to expand its work. The award is one of several reform-minded public defense initiatives funded by a $15 million Bureau of Justice Assistance grant program. So far, more than $4 million has been awarded to indigent-defense initiatives in fiscal years 2009 and 2010, up from zero in 2008. The shift within this prosecutorial-minded agency signals the [President Barack] Obama administration's seriousness about reforming public defense.

In February, Attorney General Eric Holder told lawyers at a Washington, D.C., symposium that the country's criminal defense system is "morally untenable" and "economically unsustainable," and that solutions are needed. "It must be the concern of every person who works on behalf of the public good and in the pursuit of justice," he said. The goal itself—guaranteeing that every person accused of a crime has a lawyer as competent and dedicated as Hardwick—is long overdue. But can Holder's call to action be fulfilled?

The Constitution promises the accused "the Assistance of Counsel for his defence," but the landmark case establishing the right to a state-appointed attorney for all defendants is less than 50 years old. In 1963, the U.S. Supreme Court unanimously concluded in *Gideon v. Wainwright* that the "noble ideal" of a fair trial "cannot be realized if the poor man charged with crime has to face his accusers without a lawyer to assist him."

What happened in the wake of that case was somewhat less noble. No single method of appointing counsel exists in the U.S. Instead, systems vary from state to state and even from county to county. In some jurisdictions, public defense offices pay staff a salary. In others, judges appoint attorneys who may also have a private practice, or counties hire attorneys using a low-bid contract system where a lawyer defends a set number of cases for a lump sum. In Florida and in parts of Tennessee, California, and Nebraska, top public defenders are elected in the same manner as district attorneys. Elections sound good, but the public rarely provides much oversight in the interest of criminal defendants. Some states provide 100 percent of the funding for indigent defense, some split the cost with counties, and some require counties to foot the entire bill.

The American Bar Association and the National Association for the Advancement of Colored People have chronicled the appalling outcomes of a broken system. Defendants spend excess time in jail awaiting trial—sometimes as much or more time than their eventual sentence. Overburdened or inadequately trained lawyers fail to investigate or challenge the state's evidence and instead urge plea deals. Prosecutors capitalize on weak defenses to get the accused to waive counsel and plead guilty.

"There's no oversight, no one holding providers accountable, no one removing the bad actors," says Michigan state appellate defender James Neuhard, who, through his work with the American Bar Association, has become a leader in indigent defense reform. About 40 percent of cases referred to his office are overturned on appeal because of sentencing guideline mistakes, he says. A client may have been credited with nonexistent prior convictions, for example, which automatically increased the prison term. A defense attorney with the time, training, and will to mount a serious defense, Neuhard says,

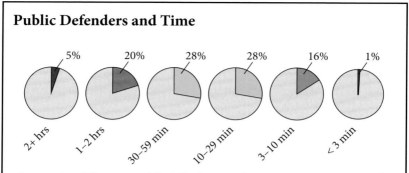

Public Defenders and Time

5%   20%   28%   28%   16%   1%

2+ hrs   1-2 hrs   30-59 min   10-29 min   3-10 min   <3 min

Average time Minnesota public defenders spend preparing witnesses to testify.

TAKEN FROM: "MinnPost Minnesota Public Defender Survey," December 13, 2010.

would easily catch such simple errors. Instead, taxpayers fund a new trial and the incarceration costs.

Tucker Carrington, director of the Mississippi Innocence Project, says that serious defense-related mistakes appear in nearly every capital case his group handles. Carrington points to an example in Lowndes County, Mississippi, where a federal judge overturned a death sentence for a man named Quintez Hodges in September. The prosecution presented false evidence during the sentencing phase, Carrington says. Hodges' advocate, his court-appointed lawyer, never bothered to test the accuracy of those claims. Instead, it took a federal judge and nine years to correct the injustice. If that kind of incompetence can happen in capital cases, Carrington says, then "you can imagine what's going on in the daily scrum of property crimes and drug offenses."

These are the kinds of cases Hardwick handles in Hinds County, and she has seen how arrests and convictions can decimate the already tenuous lives of the poor. "It's nothing for them to be arrested and in the course of that, lose their homes, furniture, clothes, jobs, spouses," she says. Most of Hardwick's clients are undereducated black men—some dropped out of school in junior high—and a dysfunctional public defense system arguably exacerbates racial injustice. But the issue is a hard sell. "There's not much of a national uproar to try to help people that are thrown into the criminal justice system and branded criminals," says Rapping of the Southern Public Defender Training Center.

And while countless dedicated lawyers represent the poor, it's no surprise that many flee for private practice. "If you spend any time in courtrooms across America, the deck is so stacked against defenders that it can have a really dispiriting, debilitating effect on you," says Knox County public defender Mark Stephens, who has worked in the field for 20 years. The median starting salary for public defenders was $46,000 in 2007, a major disincentive to law school graduates who often have six-figure debts from student loans. Hardwick's debt is about $150,000.

Like the Southern Public Defender Training Center, Stephens's office in Knoxville, Tennessee, offers another model for innovative public defending. With foundation, state, local, and federal funding, he has hired social workers, an employment counselor, and volunteers from local youth programs, which work to address the circumstances that drive people into the criminal justice system. The approach, known as holistic defense, asks lawyers to examine more than the criminal charge. It's gaining popularity but can be politically fraught. The top public defender in Maryland was fired in 2009 after being told to justify the social workers on her staff.

Stephens and other advocates, however, say it's effective. "If I don't deal with the addictions, the mental-health problems, the fact that at 14 years old your client's goal is to be a drug dealer because drug dealers make a lot of money and wear nice clothes, beating the charge won't do a thing," Stephens says. "The mistake we make as a country is we don't see public defense as the outlet to do that."

Obviously, a few forward-thinking public defenders and a skills-based training program aren't enough without institutional reform. Most observers acknowledge that there won't and shouldn't be a one-size-fits-all model for rural and urban, high-crime and low-crime jurisdictions. They generally agree, though, that states need to institute and enforce standards that ensure a defense attorney has manageable caseloads, resources, and supervision. Another critical aspect, says Jo-Ann Wallace, president and CEO of the National Legal Aid & Defender Association, is ensuring that public defenders are independent from the judiciary and report to a board or commission that focuses on policy and has oversight of the work.

Those reforms are unlikely to happen unless the federal government helps—and, if necessary, forces—states to overhaul public defending programs so that they meet a constitutionally adequate standard. Earlier this year, the Department of Justice created the Access to Justice Initiative, appointing the liberal Laurence H. Tribe, a Harvard professor and a leading legal scholar, as its head. Many reformers found both developments encouraging. "That really signaled that the Department of Justice was taking seriously this mandate to address the indigent defense crisis," says Christopher Durocher, government affairs counsel for the criminal justice program at the nonprofit Constitution Project.

The case for reform is simple, Tribe says. "Our country is dedicated to the idea that people who are accused are innocent until proven guilty and deserve a defense," he says. "And partially, it's practical: We waste an enormous amount of time and money."

Tribe's initiative can claim some early successes. The staff is working with the Bureau of Justice Statistics to collect data on indigent defense systems. This is critical for quantifying the problem and tracking what reforms work and which don't. Currently, there's a wealth of anecdotes about the broken system but few national statistics. "All of those anecdotes, when you confront a limited budget and skeptical lawmakers, they have to be backed up by data," Tribe says.

The initiative is also advising several jurisdictions in Alabama, Illinois, and Louisiana that are attempting to reform their public defending practices. In New Orleans, for example, through consultations with Tribe's staff, criminal justice professionals are designing a pretrial release program to ease the stress on jails and public defenders.

His handpicked team of six is small, and the challenges are daunting, but Tribe expects to see significant progress within a year or two.

For that to happen, however, Tribe will need Congress's assistance. The Justice for All Reauthorization Act of 2010, sponsored by Sen. Patrick Leahy of Vermont, would require the attorney general to assist states in meeting that constitutionally adequate standard. If states failed to do so, the Justice Department would have the right to sue. Lawsuits would likely be rare, but the threat is powerful. "This is sort of like what they say about [the sword of] Damocles," says Tribe, whose office helped draft the bill. "It has its effect not when it drops but just when it hangs."

Until then, poor defendants will have to rely on patchwork reforms and hope their lawyer possesses the resources and skills to mount a just defense. For her part, Hardwick continues to fight for her clients. Recently, she took the statement of Euneka Davis, whose fiancé, Thomas Stevens, was jailed on a charge of being a convicted felon in possession of a firearm.

Since receiving the case, Hardwick has tracked down the relative of one of the police witnesses, who said that the witness, her sister, is blind and that she was also drunk when she told police Stevens had a gun. Now, Hardwick sits behind her keyboard and types Davis's statement. Wiping tears away, Davis insists that she never saw Stevens with a gun on the day in question or at any other time. She adds that Stevens used to deal drugs but had changed. Before his arrest, he worked mowing lawns and trimming trees.

When they finish, Hardwick prints out a copy of the affidavit for Davis to review and sign and explains that a lie is a prosecutable felony offense. Davis reads the document in silence, then looks up at Hardwick. "This is right," she tells the public defender. "You did right."

"A voucher system will not solve every problem, but at any level of funding, defense vouchers can produce gains both for indigent defendants and for all the rest of us."

Defendants Should Have the Right to Choose Their Own Defense Attorneys

Stephen J. Schulhofer and David D. Friedman

In the following viewpoint, Stephen J. Schulhofer and David D. Friedman argue that one important way to reform the criminal defense system is to allow defendants to choose their own attorneys. The authors contend that having a public defender appointed by the state does not control the quality of defense as well as if the client made the choice. Schulhofer and Friedman claim that a voucher system would result in benefits for the defendants and for society at large. Schulhofer is the Robert B. McKay Professor of Law at New York University School of Law, and Friedman is a professor of law at Santa Clara University.

As you read, consider the following questions:

1. According to the authors, what percentage of felony defendants are poor enough to qualify for public defense?

Stephen J. Schulhofer and David D. Friedman, "Improve Legal Defense for Poor with Free-Market Solution," *Atlantic Journal-Constitution*, December 7, 2010. Copyright © 2010 by The Cato Institute. All rights reserved. Reproduced by permission.

2. Schulhofer and Friedman claim that under the current system, attorneys are selected for their ability to serve what entity?

3. What reason do the authors give for thinking that vouchers would greatly improve the quality of defense representation?

Criminal defense systems are in a state of perpetual crisis. Leading authorities surveyed by the American Bar Association portray existing arrangements as "shameful," "abysmal," "pathetic" and "deplorable." In a recent statement, former Manhattan district attorney Robert Morgenthau, along with 61 other former prosecutors, charged that indigent defense is pervaded with "systemic failures" so grave that they prevent prosecutors from fulfilling their responsibilities "to produce just outcomes that inspire public confidence." All of society has a stake in putting an end to this scandal.

The Power to Select an Attorney

In part the problem reflects inadequate resources. But there is a compounding problem that has been largely ignored: In every American jurisdiction, the person who has the most at stake—the accused—is allowed no say in choosing the professional who will provide one of the most important services he will ever need: a legal defense.

Many of the steps proposed to fix indigent defense are complex and, above all, expensive. But the system's most basic flaw could be cured by a reform that is straightforward, cheap and yet almost never considered. The power to select the defense attorney need only be transferred, by means of a voucher system, from the government to the person he or she will represent.

Indigents commonly mistrust the public defender assigned to them, viewing him as part of the same court bureaucracy that is trying to put them in prison. Nearly everyone would regard it as outrageous for one side in a civil case to have the power to appoint the other side's lawyer. And yet, in a criminal case, where the plaintiff is the state, this happens every day. If the defendant is indigent—and roughly 80 percent of felony defendants are—it is the state that selects his attorney.

A Mechanism to Control Quality

Though ample funding for indigent defense is plainly important, providing it inevitably requires tough, politically difficult choices. And even with increased resources, problems will remain in any system where the defendant's attorney is chosen for him by the state, because attorneys are likely to be selected for their ability to serve the court system. Moving cases through the process quickly might please the judge, but what about the clients who want a thorough defense of their innocence?

That foundational defect can be corrected by simply permitting the person accused of a crime to select his own attorney. That is, after all, the mechanism most of us use most of the time to control the quality of the goods and services we buy. Even if the accused cannot judge perfectly among available lawyers, at least the decision will be made by someone with an interest in making it correctly.

Counsel for indigent defendants are already paid by the government. A system of defense vouchers would permit defendants to select the lawyer who, by representing them, would earn that fee. If they preferred, defendants could choose the public defender or an attorney recommended by the court, but the choice would be theirs. Indigent defense would cost no more than at present; attorneys would be compensated in the same way as before, with either hourly fees or lump-sum payments per case.

The Benefits of Better Representation

Vouchers would greatly improve the quality of defense representation, because attorneys hoping to attract business would have to serve their clients well. Better representation will, in turn, produce at least three benefits for society. First, improving defense services will reduce the potential for mistakes. It will be less likely that innocent persons will be wrongfully convicted and less likely that the actual perpetrators will remain free to repeat their offenses.

Second, improving defense services will minimize adverse consequences even for those who would be acquitted under current systems of indigent defense. A better defense makes it more likely that the innocent will be released from custody sooner, with less disruption to their lives and less expense for the jails that hold them.

Third, improving indigent defense will bring better information to the sentencing process—making it more likely that appropriate, cost-effective punishments will be imposed on those who are guilty.

Many other countries permit indigent defendants to select the lawyers who represent them in criminal court. The province of Ontario has used defense vouchers for some time, apparently with considerable success. Of course, a voucher system will not solve every problem, but at any level of funding, defense vouchers can produce gains both for indigent defendants and for all the rest of us.

| *"Trials are one of the few things the government indisputably* should *be spending money on."*

Plea Bargaining Violates the Right to a Jury Trial

Timothy Lynch

In the following viewpoint, Timothy Lynch argues that the primary current method by which the courts handle criminal cases is to resolve them by plea bargaining, a bargaining system that he claims was never intended by the framers of the US Constitution to be a substitute for a jury trial. Lynch claims that although plea bargaining saves the government time and money, it results in the punishment of the innocent, a lack of police scrutiny, and too many lenient deals on sentencing. He concludes that something must be done to ensure criminal cases go to trial. Lynch is the director of the Cato Institute's Project on Criminal Justice.

As you read, consider the following questions:

1. According to Lynch, what percentage of criminal cases are resolved by plea bargains?

Timothy Lynch, "The Devil's Bargain: How Plea Agreements, Never Contemplated by the Framers, Undermine Justice," *Reason*, July 2011. Copyright © 2011 by The Reason Foundation. All rights reserved. Reproduced by permission.

2. From the government's perspective, what does the author identify as two advantages of plea bargaining?

3. What does Lynch identify as the most common pragmatic argument in favor of plea bargaining?

Most Americans are under the mistaken impression that when the government accuses someone of a crime, the case typically proceeds to trial, where a jury of laypeople hears arguments from the prosecution and the defense, then deliberates over the evidence before deciding on the defendant's guilt or innocence. This image of American justice is wildly off the mark. Criminal cases rarely go to trial, because about 95 percent are resolved by plea bargains. In a plea bargain, the prosecutor usually offers a reduced prison sentence if the defendant agrees to waive his right to a jury trial and admit guilt in a summary proceeding before a judge.

The Constitutional Right to a Jury Trial

This standard operating procedure was not contemplated by the framers [of the US Constitution]. The inability to enter into plea arrangements was not among the grievances set forth in the Declaration of Independence. Plea bargaining was not discussed at the Constitutional Convention or during ratification debates. In fact, the Constitution says "the Trial of all Crimes, except in Cases of Impeachment; shall be by Jury." It is evident that jury trials were supposed to play a central role in the administration of American criminal justice. But as the Yale law professor John Langbein noted in a 1992 *Harvard Journal of Law and Public Policy* article, "There is an astonishing discrepancy between what the constitutional texts promise and what the criminal justice system delivers."

No one ever proposed a radical restructuring of the criminal justice system, one that would replace jury trials with a

supposedly superior system of charge-and-sentence bargaining. Like the growth of government in general, plea bargaining slowly crept into and eventually grew to dominate the system.

Two Perspectives on Plea Bargaining

From the government's perspective, plea bargaining has two advantages. First, it's less expensive and time-consuming than jury trials, which means prosecutors can haul more people into court and legislators can add more offenses to the criminal code. Second, by cutting the jury out of the picture, prosecutors and judges acquire more influence over case outcomes.

From a defendant's perspective, plea bargaining extorts guilty pleas. People who have never been prosecuted may think there is no way they would plead guilty to a crime they did not commit. But when the government has a "witness" who is willing to lie, and your own attorney urges you to accept one year in prison rather than risk a 10-year sentence, the decision becomes harder. As William Young, then chief judge of the U.S. District Court in Massachusetts, observed in an unusually blunt 2004 opinion, "The focus of our entire criminal justice system has shifted away from trials and juries and adjudication to a massive system of sentence bargaining that is heavily rigged against the accused."

An Uncontroversial Issue

One point often stressed by progressives is that trials bring scrutiny to police conduct. But when deals are struck in courthouse hallways, judges never hear about illegal searches or detentions. This only encourages further misconduct. Conservatives, meanwhile, are right to wonder whether overburdened prosecutors give the guilty too many lenient deals. Why should an armed robber get to plead guilty to a lesser crime such as petty theft?

It is remarkable how few people will openly defend the primary method by which our courts handle criminal cases. The most common apologia for plea bargaining is a pragmatic argument: Courthouses are so busy that they would grind to a halt if every case, or even a substantial share of them, went to trial. But there is nothing inevitable about those crushing caseloads. Politicians chose to expand the list of crimes, eventually turning millions of Americans into criminals. Ending the disastrous war on drugs would unclog our courts in short order.

In any case, trials are one of the few things the government indisputably *should* be spending money on. If additional funds are needed, free them up by stopping the nation-building exercises abroad and the corporate welfare here at home. The administration of justice ought to be a top priority of government.

Periodical and Internet Sources Bibliography

The following articles have been selected to supplement the diverse views presented in this chapter.

Nick Baumann	"The New Civil Liberties Fight," *Mother Jones*, June 24, 2011.
Eric Blair	"So *Miranda* Is Hobbling Police Investigations After All," *American Spectator*, May 21, 2010.
Clay Conrad	"Indefensible: Public Defenders Are Too Overloaded to Protect the Rights of the Accused," *Reason*, July 2011.
Susan Estrich	"Competence Needed for Public Defenders," Newsmax.com, April 2, 2010.
Edward Koch	"Abolish Miranda Rights," Newsmax.com, May 18, 2010.
Matthew Rothschild	"A Horrendous Decision on Habeas Corpus," *Progressive*, January 9, 2010.
Paul H. Rubin	"The Exclusionary Rule's Hidden Costs," *Wall Street Journal*, February 28, 2009.
Charles D. Stimson and James Jay Carafano	"Treating Terrorism Solely as a Law Enforcement Matter—Not Miranda—Is the Problem," Heritage Foundation, May 13, 2010. www.heritage.org.
Geoffrey R. Stone	"Missing the Point: Terrorism and Miranda," *Huffington Post*, May 17, 2010. www.huffingtonpost.com.
Stuart Taylor Jr.	"Holder's Promising Interrogation Plan," *National Journal*, May 22, 2010.
Bruce Western	"Decriminalizing Poverty," *Nation*, December 27, 2010.

For Further Discussion

Chapter 1

1. Sasha Abramsky and Nastassia Walsh have different opinions on the role of drug courts. What is one point of agreement between the two? Explain.

2. Marc Mauer and John Perazzo have contradictory opinions on the presence of racial discrimination in the criminal justice system. How might Mauer respond to Perazzo's claim that unequal arrest rates between blacks and whites simply reflect dissimilar rates of engagement in criminal acts?

Chapter 2

1. The viewpoints of James Q. Wilson and Bruce Western both have a different assessment of the link between more incarceration and less crime. Place the viewpoints on a spectrum from the one that maintains the bigger link to the one that asserts the smaller. Back up your answer with specific information from the viewpoints.

2. Patrice Gaines, the editors of *America*, and Thomas Sowell have different opinions on the proper role of incarceration in the criminal justice system. Explain how the three viewpoints differ in their approach to the issue based on importance of cost.

Chapter 3

1. John W. Whitehead objects to the death penalty primarily because of the risk of error; he says there is no deterrent effect. But David Muhlhausen argues in favor of the death penalty, claiming that, in fact, the risk of this punishment does deter potential criminals and saves lives. Assume both authors are partially correct—that innocent people

are executed each year and also that the threat of the death penalty saves lives. What principle could one use to resolve the issue of whether or not the death penalty should be allowed?

2. Several of the authors in this chapter discuss the efficacy of harsh sentences. List the authors in order from the advocate of the greatest severity of punishment to the advocate of the least severity, briefly identifying the justification for each position.

Chapter 4

1. Charles Krauthammer argues that terrorists should not be given Miranda warnings until all information regarding public safety is acquired. What would the editors of *America* respond to his argument? Explain.

2. Vanessa Gregory expresses concern that the poor are not getting adequate legal representation under the current public defense system. Stephen J. Schulhofer and David D. Friedman argue that a voucher system where defendants choose their attorneys would help reform the system. Do you think Gregory would welcome their reform? Why or why not?

Organizations to Contact

The editors have compiled the following list of organizations concerned with the issues debated in this book. The descriptions are derived from materials provided by the organizations. All have publications or information available for interested readers. The list was compiled on the date of publication of the present volume; the information provided here may change. Be aware that many organizations take several weeks or longer to respond to inquiries, so allow as much time as possible.

American Bar Association (ABA)
740 Fifteenth Street NW, Washington, DC 20005-1019
(202) 662-1000 • fax: (202) 662-1501
website: www.abanet.org

The American Bar Association (ABA) is a voluntary membership organization for professionals within the legal field that provides law school accreditation and works to promote justice, excellence of those within the legal profession, and respect for the law. The Criminal Justice Section of the ABA is dedicated to maintaining the integrity of criminal justice law and providing information on the state of the criminal justice system in the United States. *Criminal Justice* is the quarterly magazine of this section of the ABA, which also publishes an annual report on the state of the criminal justice system in America.

American Civil Liberties Union (ACLU)
125 Broad Street, 18th Floor, New York, NY 10004
(212) 549-2500
e-mail: infoaclu@aclu.org
website: www.aclu.org

The American Civil Liberties Union (ACLU) is a national organization that works to defend Americans' civil rights as outlined in the US Constitution. The ACLU works in courts, legislatures, and communities to defend First Amendment rights, the right to equal protection, the right to due process, and the right to privacy. The ACLU publishes the semiannual newsletter *Civil Liberties Alert*, as well as briefing papers including the report "Locking Up Our Children."

American Enterprise Institute for Public Policy Research (AEI)
1150 Seventeenth Street NW, Washington, DC   20036
(202) 862-5800 • fax: (202) 862-7177
website: www.aei.org

The American Enterprise Institute for Public Policy Research (AEI) is a private, nonpartisan, not-for-profit institution dedicated to research and education on issues of government, politics, economics, and social welfare. AEI sponsors research and publishes materials with the goal of defending the principles and improving the institutions of American freedom and democratic capitalism. AEI publishes the *AEI Outlook Series* and the online magazine the *American*.

Amnesty International
5 Penn Plaza, 16th Floor, New York, NY   10001
(212) 807-8400 • fax: (212) 463-9193
e-mail: admin-us@aiusa.org
website: www.amnesty.org

Amnesty International is a worldwide movement of people who campaign for global human rights. Amnesty International conducts research and generates action to prevent and end abuses of human rights and to demand justice for those whose rights have been violated. Amnesty International opposes the death penalty. Among the publications available at its website is the report on the death penalty in the United States that notes concerns about racism, "30 Years of Executions, 30 Years of Wrongs."

Cato Institute
1000 Massachusetts Avenue NW
Washington, DC 20001-5403
(202) 842-0200 • fax: (202) 842-3490
website: www.cato.org

The Cato Institute is a public policy research organization dedicated to the principles of individual liberty, limited government, free markets, and peace. The Cato Institute is dedicated to increasing and enhancing the understanding of key public policies and realistically analyzing their impact on the principles identified above. The Cato Institute publishes many journals and reports, such as the quarterly *Regulation* magazine, the bimonthly *Cato Policy Report*, and the periodic *Cato Journal*.

Families Against Mandatory Minimums (FAMM)
1100 H Street NW, Suite 1000, Washington, DC 20005
(202) 822-6700 • fax: (202) 822-6704
website: www.famm.org

Families Against Mandatory Minimums (FAMM) works to educate the government and the public about what it sees as the unfairness and negative impact of mandatory minimum sentencing. FAMM advocates for state and federal sentencing reform and works to mobilize thousands of individuals and families whose lives are adversely affected by unjust sentences. Reports and papers outlining the history of mandatory minimums and their impact, as well as information on FAMM's current activities, are available on the organization's website.

Heritage Foundation
214 Massachusetts Avenue NE, Washington, DC 20002-4999
(202) 546-4400 • fax: (202) 546-8328
e-mail: info@heritage.org
website: www.heritage.org

The Heritage Foundation is a conservative public policy organization dedicated to promoting policies that align with the principles of free enterprise, limited government, individual freedom, traditional American values, and a strong national defense. The Heritage Foundation conducts research on policy issues for members of Congress, key congressional staff members, policy makers, the nation's news media, and the academic and policy communities. The Heritage Foundation has hundreds of reports, fact sheets, testimonies, and commentaries available at its website concerning the issue of criminal justice.

Human Rights Watch (HRW)
350 Fifth Avenue, 34th Floor, New York, NY   10118-3299
(212) 290-4700 • fax: (212) 736-1300
e-mail: hrwnyc@hrw.org
website: www.hrw.org

Human Rights Watch (HRW) is dedicated to protecting the human rights of people around the world. HRW investigates human rights abuses, educates the public, and works to change policy and practice. Among its numerous publications is the report "Targeting Blacks: Drug Law Enforcement and Race in the United States."

Justice Policy Institute (JPI)
1012 Fourteenth Street NW, Suite 400
Washington, DC   20005
(202) 558-7974 • fax: (202) 558-7978
e-mail: info@justicepolicy.org
website: www.justicepolicy.org

The Justice Policy Institute (JPI) is a national nonprofit organization that aims to reduce the use of incarceration and the justice system, as well as promote policies that improve the well-being of all people and communities. JPI identifies effective programs and policies and disseminates their findings to the media, policy makers, and advocates. JPI's reports, briefs, and fact sheets are available at its website, among which is the report "System Overload: The Costs of Under-Resourcing Public Defense."

National Institute of Justice (NIJ)
810 Seventh Street NW, Washington, DC 20531
(202) 307-2942
website: www.nij.gov

The National Institute of Justice (NIJ), a component of the Office of Justice Programs, US Department of Justice, is dedicated to improving knowledge and understanding of crime and justice issues through scientific methodology. NIJ provides objective and independent knowledge and tools to reduce crime and promote justice, particularly at the state and local levels. NIJ publishes the monthly *NIJ Journal*, along with numerous studies, all of which is available at its website.

Office of Juvenile Justice and Delinquency Prevention (OJJDP)
810 Seventh Street NW, Washington, DC 20531
(202) 307-5911
website: www.ojjdp.gov

The Office of Juvenile Justice and Delinquency Prevention (OJJDP), a component of the Office of Justice Programs, US Department of Justice, collaborates with professionals from diverse disciplines to improve juvenile justice policies and practices. OJJDP accomplishes its mission by supporting states, local communities, and tribal jurisdictions in their efforts to develop and implement effective programs for juveniles. Through its Juvenile Justice Clearinghouse, OJJDP provides access to fact sheets, summaries, reports, and articles from its journal *Juvenile Justice.*

RAND Corporation
1776 Main Street, Santa Monica, CA 90401-3208
(310) 393-0411 • fax: (310) 393-4818
website: www.rand.org

The RAND Corporation is a nonprofit organization that conducts research on complicated social problems. The RAND Corporation's Drug Policy Research Center conducts research to help community leaders and public officials develop more effective ways of dealing with drug problems. *DPRC Insights* is a regularly published electronic newsletter that focuses on major drug policy issues.

The Sentencing Project
1705 DeSales Street NW, 8th Floor, Washington, DC   20036
(202) 628-0871 • fax: (202) 628-1091
e-mail: staff@sentencingproject.org
website: www.sentencingproject.org

The Sentencing Project is a national organization working for a fair and effective criminal justice system. The Sentencing Project promotes reforms in sentencing law and practice, as well as promotes alternatives to incarceration. The Sentencing Project produces publications on a wide range of issues, including sentencing policy, racial disparity, felony disenfranchisement, and women in the justice system.

United States Department of Justice (USDOJ)
950 Pennsylvania Avenue NW, Washington, DC   20530-0001
(202) 514-2000
e-mail: AskDOJ@usdoj.gov
website: www.usdoj.gov

The US Department of Justice (USDOJ) is the office of the US government charged with upholding the laws of the United States in order to protect the country as a whole. Agencies of the USDOJ include the Office of Justice Programs, the Drug Enforcement Administration (DEA), and the Bureau of Prisons. USDOJ publishes the annual *Uniform Crime Report* and other publications containing statistics on crime, punishment, and justice.

United States Sentencing Commission (USSC)
One Columbus Circle NE, Suite 2-500
Washington, DC   20002-8002
(202) 502-4500

e-mail: pubaffairs@ussc.gov
website: www.ussc.gov

The United States Sentencing Commission (USSC) is an independent agency in the judicial branch of the government. USSC establishes sentencing policies and practices for the federal courts; advises and assists Congress and the executive branch in the development of effective and efficient crime policy; and collects, analyzes, researches, and distributes a broad array of information on federal crime and sentencing issues. USSC publishes quarterly and annual reports on federal sentencing statistics that are available at its website.

Bibliography of Books

Michelle Alexander — *The New Jim Crow: Mass Incarceration in the Age of Colorblindness.* New York: New Press, 2010.

James Austin and John Irwin — *It's About Time: America's Imprisonment Binge.* Belmont, CA: Wadsworth Publishing, 2012.

Robert M. Baird and Stuart E. Rosenbaum, eds. — *The Death Penalty: Debating the Moral, Legal, and Political Issues.* Amherst, NY: Prometheus Books, 2011.

Howard Ball — *Bush, the Detainees, and the Constitution: The Battle over Presidential Power in the War on Terror.* Lawrence, KS: University Press of Kansas, 2007.

Gregg Barak, Paul Leighton, and Jeanne Flavin — *Class, Race, Gender, and Crime: The Social Realities of Justice in America.* Lanham, MD: Rowman & Littlefield, 2010.

Greg Berman and Aubrey Fox — *Trial & Error in Criminal Justice Reform: Learning from Failure.* Washington, DC: Urban Institute Press, 2010.

Mary Bosworth — *Explaining U.S. Imprisonment.* Los Angeles, CA: Sage, 2010.

Michael Braswell, Larry Miller, and Joycelyn Pollock — *Case Studies in Criminal Justice Ethics.* Long Grove, IL: Waveland Press, 2012.

Dean John Champion, Alida V. Merlo, and Peter J. Benekos	*The Juvenile Justice System: Delinquency, Processing, and the Law.* Upper Saddle River, NJ: Pearson Education, 2013.
George F. Cole and Christopher E. Smith	*Criminal Justice in America.* Belmont, CA: Wadsworth Cengage Learning, 2011.
Kevin Davis	*Defending the Damned: Inside Chicago's Cook County Public Defender's Office.* New York: Atria, 2007.
Jamie L. Flexon	*Racial Disparities in Capital Sentencing: Prejudice and Discrimination in the Jury Room.* El Paso, TX: LFB Scholarly Publishing, 2012.
Larry K. Gaines and Roger LeRoy Miller	*Criminal Justice in Action: The Core.* Belmont, CA: Wadsworth Cengage Learning, 2011.
Karen S. Glover	*Racial Profiling: Research, Racism, and Resistance.* Lanham, MD: Rowman & Littlefield, 2009.
Jack Goldsmith	*The Terror Presidency: Law and Judgment Inside the Bush Administration.* New York: W.W. Norton & Co., 2007.
David L. Hudson, Jr.	*Juvenile Justice.* New York: Chelsea House Publishers, 2010.
James A. Inciardi	*Criminal Justice.* Boston, MA: McGraw-Hill Higher Education, 2009.

David W. Neubauer and Henry F. Fradella — *America's Courts and the Criminal Justice System.* Belmont, CA: Wadsworth Cengage Learning, 2012.

Joycelyn M. Pollock — *Ethical Dilemmas and Decisions in Criminal Justice.* Belmont, CA: Wadsworth Cengage Learning, 2012.

Jeffrey Reiman and Paul Leighton — *The Rich Get Richer and the Poor Get Prison: Ideology, Class, and Criminal Justice.* Boston, MA: Pearson, 2013.

Frank Schmalleger — *Criminal Justice: A Brief Introduction.* Boston, MA: Prentice Hall, 2012.

Larry J. Siegel and John L. Worrall — *Essentials of Criminal Justice.* Belmont, CA: Wadsworth Cengage Learning, 2013.

William J. Stuntz — *The Collapse of American Criminal Justice.* Cambridge, MA: Belknap Press, 2011.

Anthony C. Thompson — *Releasing Prisoners, Redeeming Communities: Reentry, Race, and Politics.* New York: New York University Press, 2008.

Gennaro F. Vito and Julie C. Kunselman — *Juvenile Justice Today.* Boston, MA: Prentice Hall, 2012.

Samuel Walker, Cassia Spohn, and Miriam DeLone — *The Color of Justice: Race, Ethnicity, and Crime in America.* Belmont, CA: Wadsworth Publishing, 2012.

Index

A

Abdulmutallab, Umar Farouk, 168–169, 171, 176

Abortion, and crime rates, 78

Abramsky, Sasha, 19, 31–38

Access to Justice Initiative, 184

Addison, Antonio, 96

African Americans
  crime rates, 51, 58, 61, 63, 70, 72, 76–78, 87
  death row, 114, 118–120
  drug use rates, 52, 77–78
  incarceration length, 141
  incarceration rates (disproportionately high), 50, 51, 57, 82, 141
  incarceration rates (not disproportionately high), 59, 61–62

Age of consent laws, 14–15

Ahmadinejad, Mahmoud, 112

AIDS rates, 83

Airline terrorism, 23, 24, 168–169, 171, 176

al-Qaeda, conspirators, 25–26

Alabama
  life without parole, 140, 143, 145
  public defense system, 185

Alaska
  life without parole policy, 140, 143
  public defense system spending, 179

Allegheny County Jail, 17

Alternative courts, 19, 31, 34, 38
  cost savings, 31, 33, 34, 36–37, 45, 46–47, 48
  costs are higher, 42, 44, 45, 47
  expansion, 37
  See also Drug courts; Health courts

Alternatives to incarceration
  high costs, 102–105
  pretrial release programs, 185
  probation and parole, 98–101, 154–155
  problem-solving courts (constance), 39–48
  problem-solving courts (pro-stance), 31–38
  restorative justice, 90–97

America (periodical)
  probation and parole are good alternatives to incarceration, 98–101
  terrorist suspects should have right to Miranda warnings, 167–171

American Bar Association, on public defenders, 53, 181, 188

American Civil Liberties Union (ACLU), 113

American colonial law, 126–127

Americans in prison, 68, 81–82, 91, 138, 151
  See also Prison populations

Amnesty International, 111

Anger management, 96

Antipoverty programs, 88–89, 114–115

N